UNMOVED
CHESS PIECES

*A simple comedian is forced to
confront the game of life and death*

Written by
Ed Driscoll

CHAPTER ONE

"Hey, how's it going? I'm Gene Hibb, with Endeavor Talent Agency."

The eager twenty-something extended his hand, and I reciprocated.

"Nice to meet you, Gene. I---"

"Wow, great party, huh?" he interrupted.

"Ooh, listen, you don't want to call it a 'party,'" I deadpanned. "You might upset the host. He put a lot of money and effort into this. Well, he put the money in, his staff put in the effort. But you'd better call it a 'reception,' not a 'party.' Otherwise, you could get kicked out of here."

Gene looked around at the A-list of actors, directors, musicians, and agents that wandered the grounds of the famed executive producer's estate, then lowered his voice. "Right, I don't want to tick anybody off."

"Too late," I joked. He looked at me quizzically. Man, if there was any more of a disconnection with this guy, we'd be dating.

"So, you're an agent at Endeavor, huh?" I
asked.

"Yeah, well, junior agent, actually, but on
my way up. You know, our agency is really
hot. We represent a lot of great people."

"Oh, yeah? Like who?"

"Well, you know, some biggies like Denzell
Washington, and Aaron Sorkin, and some
other guys that are not as recognizable but
are great, like Ed Driscoll."

I raised an eyebrow. "You represent Ed
Driscoll?"

"Oh, yeah," he nodded. "You know him?"

"I *am* Ed Driscoll."

The young agent went completely white.

"Oh, wow, Ed Driscoll, yeah, man, I'm sorry,
I didn't recognize you!"

"That's okay, Gene, I didn't recognize you
either."

He laughed nervously. "So, congrats on all
your success."

I smiled. My career as a comedian, writer,
and producer continued to rise steadily,
often in spite of myself.   "Thanks, Gene,

2

and it's nice to meet you. I'm going to mingle a bit."

"Uh, yeah, well, me too."

"But maybe you'd better get a set of agency picture flash cards, just in case you run into any more clients."

Gene laughed sheepishly and disappeared into the throng of people dropping shrimp onto their plates. I shook my head and looked around for my manager Ahmos. I couldn't wait to tell him about this classic Hollywood encounter.

The party was filled with the nervous energy that typically accompanied this time of year known as "pilot season," when new television shows are contracted, developed, and shot, which is what I often felt they should do to some of the executives making the decisions.

I found Ahmos talking shop with some folks from Warner Brothers studios near the pat'e sculpted to look like an old-fashioned movie projector.

"Hey, Ed, a bunch of the top guys at Warner Brothers caught you on "Politically Incorrect" and loved it. They want you to do some joke punch-up on the new "Scooby Doo" movie."

"Rell, that's rate, raggy," I said in my worst Scooby voice.

"Yeah, I don't think you'll be doing any voice-overs for them," Ahmos teased.

"Wow, pretty productive party for you, Ahmos. The best I did was meet some guy who told me he represents me."

"Oh, that Gene guy? Yeah, I talked to him, too. A nice fella, but a little green."

"A *little* green? Right, so's the Hulk."

Ahmos laughed. "Anyway, I talked to the HBO folks, too, and they're looking forward to the project you're bringing to them."

"Great," I said, "That will be a fun one to do as my last gig in this town."

Ahmos turned serious. "So you're still intent on moving back to Pittsburgh, huh?"

"Yes," I answered quietly.

Though I hadn't announced this decision to anyone, not even my own family, it was not one that I'd arrived at on a whim. In truth, I was grateful for the way my comedy career had taken off, bringing me awards and national television appearances, and a comfortable living. But I had just turned forty, and had started feeling a bit restless about my life and career. Somewhere in my mind I realized that I was far from old, but forty certainly was a milestone where most people take some kind of stock of where they are in their lives, and compare it to where they'd expected, or at least wanted, to be.

It sure had been an interesting ride for me over the last decade, from finally confronting my alcohol problem, to confronting my "dealing with life sober" problem, to still trying to solve my "lack of a meaningful relationship with a woman" problem. I'd gotten close to dealing with that last one shortly after I'd moved to LA, when I got engaged to a woman named

Rita. Unfortunately, that relationship broke up just a few months before the wedding date. At least I wasn't left at the alter. It was more like I was tossed from the speeding limo onto the highway outside the church.

I missed my family back in Western Pennsylvania. I'm the youngest of four children, which makes me the baby of the family. Actually, my behavior makes me the baby of the family, being the youngest just makes me the youngest. I felt so far away from my family and many of my dearest friends who still resided back East.

One of the toughest things about my break-up with my fiancée was losing not only her, but her family. Her parents had become my surrogate parents, and the emptiness I felt when I split with Rita was intensified by the loss of my "west coast family."

In fact, when I first told my agent about Rita and me calling it quits, he exclaimed, "Wow, I'll bet you've got some hilarious stuff about it!" Not exactly the sort of comforting comment I was looking for. But I realized he did have a point, and I immediately set about writing a new one-hour stand-up show entitled "Mismatch Maker," which would deal entirely with the difficulties of trying to meet the right woman in such an odd, transient town as LA. I was expecting to open the show in Hollywood sometime in the next few months. However, I hoped that I didn't have to keep going through heart-breaking relationships just to get new material.

Though the eight years I'd been in Hollywood had been good to me in many ways, I never quite felt as though I fit in. I always had a nagging fear that I was losing myself in the constant, dizzying swirl of the Hollywood lifestyle. I'd managed to keep my basic good values that I'd learned from my parents, but the somewhat necessary reliance on artificial people, places, and relationships that Hollywood engenders was inescapable, and I felt like it was beginning to take a toll on me.

While friends of mine often wistfully spoke of living in LA like me, I often spoke wistfully of living a "real" life back in Pittsburgh, like them. As they envied the "glamour" of attending the Oscars, performing on television, and frequenting parties with famous people, I envied their "normalcy" of raising families, going to Steelers games, and gathering on weekends to play cards and gossip about what was happening in the neighborhood. I guess it's a perfect example of "the grass is always greener," except that the greenery in California frequently catches fire.

Ever since I had moved into one of the more "residential" areas of LA, I had always hoped for a neighborhood experience like the one I knew growing up in Pittsburgh. Back east, everyone on our street knew everyone, and everyone looked after each other. In LA, people look *out* for each other, as in, "look out for those weird people in that house across the street, the cops are there every other day."

There are lots of people who migrate to LA from the East, and they're usually looking to re-create that sense of community they were so familiar with. So realtors in LA commonly try to sell houses with the promise that "it's in a neighborhood that's just like back East!" What they fail to mention is, they mean East Fallujah.

When I was shopping for my first house in California some ten years ago, my realtor Paula, a botoxed, fake-tanned woman who was also a "part-time actress," told me "You absolutely *must* live in a gated community."

"Why's that?" I asked.

"Because there's no better way to live!" she chirped.

"Yeah, tell it to the fellas at Leavenworth," I answered.

She looked at me a moment, and said, "I've heard about that town, it's near Santa Monica, right?"

Clearly, the botox had enlarged her lips, but nothing on the inside of her head.

"Actually, it's near Van Nuys," I replied. Call it a gut instinct, but I went with another realtor, and ultimately bought a place that had about as much of a neighborhood feel as I could find. But it didn't take long to discover that things weren't quite like I'd hoped.

One of the first days after I moved into my house, I was trimming some bushes in the front yard when an older man on a bicycle rolled by on the sidewalk. Suddenly, he jammed on his brakes, going from one mile per hour to zero on a dime, and looked at me. That's all. He didn't wave, he didn't smile, he didn't say anything...he just stopped and stared at me.

After a few excruciatingly long moments, I realized that apparently only I was uncomfortable with this situation.

Clearly I would have to be the one to break the ice.

"Hi, I'm Ed," I offered.

"Did you just move in here?" he replied.

"Well, nice to meet you, Mr. 'Did you just move in here'..." was my first thought, but since I was new to the area, I decided to be polite.

"Yes, I moved in a couple days ago."

"Huh. What did you pay for it?"

Wow, there you have it. I understand most people are curious about such things, as am I. In fact, I'm often curious as to what kind of salary people make at their jobs, how old they are, and what they weigh. But that doesn't mean I ASK THEM. This guy must have just come from his doctor's office, fresh from a tact-otomy.

Slightly startled, I tried to make a joke out of it. Pointing to my hedge clippers, I leaned in to him and whispered conspiratorially, "I paid twenty bucks at Orchard Hardware. Don't tell anybody else, okay?" I smiled, and he stared at me blankly for a moment.

"I meant the house, how much did you pay for your house?"

Okay, he wasn't catching my drift, so I guess I'd have to be as blunt as he was.

"Well, I don't really like discussing things like that," I said, then tried to change the subject.

"Do you live nearby?" I inquired.

"Yeah, a couple streets over."

And that was it. I looked at him expectantly, like he might actually say the name of the street or something like that, but no. It was back to the soulless stare.

He pointed to a small bit of paint peeling on a beam near my roof, and said, "Looks like it's pretty run down."

Wow again. While doctors may indeed have removed his tact, they surely found there's nothing wrong with his balls.

"Well, that's nice of you to say," I finally replied.

He grunted, then said, "I heard someone from the studios bought this house. Do you work for the studios?"

Beautiful. All I'd wanted to do was relax and trim some hedges, and now I was being grilled by the president of the local "unwelcome" wagon.

"Sometimes I work at the studios, yeah."

"Hey, my daughter is looking for a studio job. Can you help her?"

All I could do was admire the sheer gall of this guy. My first thought was, "*Yeah, if you could just ask a couple more rude questions, then ridicule my house a bit more, I'll hire her today!!*" But again, I wanted to remain polite, so what I actually said was, "No."

He looked at me for a moment, then said, "Well, it's a pretty cliquey business you guys have, huh?"

And before I could answer, he pedaled away. Gosh, just like Mayberry. I was just relieved that he didn't live right next door to me.

A few days after that, I was planting a couple small bushes next to my driveway when I was suddenly confronted in a hostile manner by what appeared to be a female human, though I'm not positive. She resembled Jabba the Hut, without the pleasant demeanor or commitment to a healthy lifestyle.

"Hey, are you living here now?" she barked at me.

"Yes, I just moved in. I'm Ed."

She nodded her head, somewhat suspiciously. "I'm Henrietta. I live next door."

"Nice to meet you," I said warmly.

"The people that lived here before, I didn't like them," she announced.

Yes, I thought, I'm sure it was *they* who were the problem.

"Well, that's too bad. I hope you'll like me," I said.

"I hope so, too." She pointed at the ground where I was working.

"Do you know what type of plants you're putting in there?"

I looked down. "The guy at the garden center said it's something called 'poison ivy' or 'sumac,' something like that," I kidded. She looked at me with irritation. Man, this seemed to be a bad area for a comedian to live. Another interaction like this with the locals, and I'll start believing I don't have a funny bone in my body. Not good for the confidence.

"Actually, I can't remember what the guy told me, but they're just nice little plants." She grimaced. "Well, that's fine if that's all they are. Because they're pretty close to my front porch, and if they grow big roots, they could undermine my property."

I laughed until I realized she wasn't kidding. "Oh, well, um, I don't think they will grow that fast or wildly. I didn't buy them from a villager named Jack."

She snorted and left. I finished putting the plants in, all the while trying to figure out

15

just what in the world that little exchange had been all about.

That night my doorbell rang, and I answered it to find a glowering Henrietta. "I took a couple leaves from your plant to the garden store and had them analyzed in their lab," she began ominously.

'Analyzed in the lab?' What is this, 'CSI: Burbank?'

Before I could even process this bizarre bit of information, she continued.

"They told me those plants of yours have some of the longest growing roots in that species."

"Well, I do want to lay down roots here in California," I offered.

"Listen," she snapped, "I'd appreciate it if you'll plant something else there instead."

At this point, I was contemplating planting *her* in the garden. Although from her strange dye job, I could see that she had long roots, too. Just how fast did she think my plants would be growing, anyway? It would probably take several decades for them to even come near her property, and she was at least seventy years old. Did she expect to live forever? Considering she seemed to be a witch, she probably did. However, in the interest of peace in my new neighborhood, I told her I'd be glad to put in some other type of plant. She gave a satisfied nod, then said, "I had no choice but to check those plants, for all I know, it could have been marijuana."

If you're looking for dope, why don't you check your mirror, I thought to myself, but didn't say anything. She abruptly turned and marched back to her house, leaving me suddenly longing for a visit from the "place looks rundown" guy. By comparison, I'd judged his credentials as a good neighbor too harshly.

All this fun was just in my first week of living in my new "neighborhood." Things hadn't gotten much friendlier in the four years since.

Speaking of plants and leaves, another thing I missed from back east, aside from basic civility, was the change of seasons. Okay, maybe not Winter so much, but the Fall, definitely. However, every October, my mom would mail me some colorful leaves from our front yard in Pittsburgh, so that I wouldn't miss out on the season entirely.

I occasionally vocalized a desire to return to a regular life in Pittsburgh, but nobody ever took me seriously, including my family. Only Ahmos knew how serious I was. Well, he and the realtor who was now shopping my house around.

Ahmos often seemed to be as torn as I was, both about my life, and his. He also was from the "Midwest," which in LA means anyplace that isn't LA or New York. He hailed from Grand Blanc, Michigan, and had grown up with many of the same family-oriented values I had. On the one hand, he understood me wanting to be back home in Pennsylvania, just as he occasionally pined to be back in Michigan. On the other hand, he knew what a good thing we had going out here, and was sad to think I'd want to end it. But being more than a representative to me, he was a true friend, and was always supportive of anything I wanted to do, even if he didn't necessarily agree with it.

Back at the LA party, Ahmos pulled me aside.
"Hey, you can't leave town just yet. After all, I'm still trying to get that run for 'Mismatch Maker.' Let's talk about it."
I glanced at my watch. "Can we talk about it on the phone? I have to take off for my, you know...appointment."
"Oh, your shrink?" Ahmos inquired loudly.
"Yes!" I whispered, giving him a look.
"She's probably here somewhere," Ahmos said.
"God, I hope not. I'm gonna get out of here before some woman approaches me and

says she's Ed Driscoll's shrink. I'll call you on my drive there."

I dashed to the front of the house, got my car from the valet, and began winding my way down the snaking canyon roads leading to Beverly Hills. Naturally, even on a Saturday afternoon, I immediately found myself in the midst of the omnipresent LA traffic jam. I dialed up Ahmos.

"Man, you should see this traffic," I whined.

"That's LA. Where else do you see eight lanes, none of them moving?"

"At the DMV?" I offered.

"You see, Ed, that kind of wit is why you'll remain a slave to Hollywood whether you want to or not."

"Gosh, thanks for the compliment. So, how's it going there? Is the party managing to continue even without me?"

"Hey, they don't even know you're gone."

"Exactly how it will be when I move back to Pittsburgh."

We chatted about some upcoming meetings for a bit, then said goodbye as I made my way down Coldwater Canyon. Really, we didn't say "Goodbye," because nobody in LA actually says "Goodbye," you just talk until the signal is cut off by one of the canyons.

I pulled into the parking lot in Beverly Hills, parking in the only space left, wedged between two SUVs the size of firetrucks. As I walked to my shrink's office, my cell phone rang again. It was Ahmos.

"Hey, sorry to be the bearer of bad news," he began.

"That's okay, I'm often the bearer of bad jokes. What's up?"

It turned out that Ahmos had just spoken to a producer who'd hired me to co-host a television show, along with two other guys, scheduled for shooting in Venezuela in a few weeks. At one point, this producer had asked me to recommend someone who could write for the show, as well as do

21

some on-camera work. I'd recommended a friend of mine, who they'd been reluctant to hire, but I'd pushed for him because I knew that he needed the work. Now, they'd decided to cut the budget significantly because of production cost overruns, so they were not using me or the other two guys as hosts. They were using...my friend that I'd pushed on them against their will. Apparently, this had been decided a week ago, but neither the producer nor my friend had called to inform me. The only reason we knew now was because Ahmos had run into my friend's wife at the reception, and she'd told him how excited she was that her husband was hosting this show in Venezuela. Ahmos then called the producer to confront him about this, and he admitted it was all true, and that he just hadn't felt up to telling us.

"You know, Ahmos, I don't even really care about the gig. I wasn't particularly psyched to leave the country and increase my chances of showing up on some terrorist website getting beheaded. But the fact that they didn't have the decency to tell me is truly inexcusable."

"I can't believe your friend didn't call you."

"Yeah, well, that's the show biz family for you. Hard to believe I want to go back to Pittsburgh, isn't it?" I muttered. "And here I was afraid I wouldn't have anything to talk to my shrink about."

Just as I entered the office building, my cell rang yet again.

Now what? Maybe the cops were calling to tell me that some other "friend" I'd tried to get work for had stolen my ATM card and was draining my bank account. I glanced at the caller ID, and saw it was my mom. I pushed the talk button.

"Oh, hi Mom, I'm on my way to...uh, the doctor...no, nothing's wrong, just having them check my...head. Just some headaches, you know, not a big deal at all. What's up?"

"Your father fell again. He's in the hospital."

Apparently, Dad had required quite a few stitches in his head when he'd fallen while trying to replace a lightbulb in a particularly precarious section of the garage. It was another example of him trying to do everything himself, as he had for years, but it was a very tough task to deal with those particular bulbs. They were tucked at an odd angle, and I remember barely being able to replace them when I was a flexible teenager. You could bring a performer from Cirque de Soleil into that garage, and he'd say, "Sorry, I can't squeeze myself into that little space." Yet, somehow Dad felt it should be no problem for a man with two hips more fragile than a middle east peace treaty.

My ears were popping like a string of firecrackers. I put down the travel chess computer I was playing and stretched my arms out over my head. The plane was beginning its descent into Pittsburgh, and as it banked into its final turn, I looked out over the city and smiled. I always liked coming back to my hometown, even under these less-than-ideal circumstances. I realized I had to convince my parents that they needed to sell the house. It was just too big for two people, especially two people in their early eighties. Too many sharp-angled staircases, typical of Pittsburgh architecture. My dad, though in excellent mental health, had begun a steady physical decline the last few years. He'd developed a case of severe arthritis in his hips, and it was getting tougher and tougher for him to walk. Only recently, he'd been forced to stop playing golf, because he couldn't make the proper body turn. I too had recently been forced to quit golf, not because of any physical limitations, but because I suck at it, and was tired of being thrashed by every snot-nosed kid at the local country club.

Having been an engineer for United States Steel for his entire professional life, Dad possessed a keen mind, and always had a variety of interests. He was a voracious reader, made furniture, worked on the car, played golf, loved to swim. However, this recent hobby of falling and busting bones needed to stop. He continued to act as though he were, well, my age, instead of eighty-three. He was still cutting the yard himself. Hell, I'm half that age and I don't cut my own yard! I hire one of the snot-nosed kids who kicks my ass in golf.

To complicate things further, Dad was too stubborn to use a cane, though he desperately needed one. He felt it wasn't "dignified," yet in a restaurant, he'd steady himself by grabbing the backs of people's chairs as he made his way to his table rather than rely on a cane. Somehow, this seemed more dignified to him.

Mom was becoming more and more concerned about Dad's spills, this being the first one that landed him in the hospital, though he'd had at least a half-dozen that probably *should* have brought him to the hospital. As always, he insisted he was okay, and that "emergency rooms are for emergencies." I guess an elderly guy splitting his head like a cord of firewood doesn't qualify as an "emergency." Boy, I wish I'd inherited my dad's toughness in this regard. If I get so much as a papercut, I'm on the phone with paramedics. When I broke my finger playing football as a teenager, there wasn't a soul in the neighborhood who didn't hear about it from me. "You're quite the silent sufferer, Eddie," Mom would always tease.

I grabbed my luggage from the overhead rack and headed down the ramp and out into the unseasonably warm April afternoon. Because of the security measures, I always try to pack as lightly as possible. I must have a suspicious look about me or something because I'm always singled out for a search. I always have to step off to the side, and as some guy with a bag of machetes saunters through unmolested, they strip me naked and run a Geiger counter over my pocket comb. Oh, well, if it makes it safer for my fellow travelers, I guess I can do my part.

I ruminated over the family meeting that my sisters and I had agreed must take place. Oddly, we're all five years apart; Keira, fifty-five, Caitlin, fifty, Melissa, forty-five, and myself now at the dreaded four-oh. I'm not sure if it was planned like that or not, and it certainly wasn't something I'd have the temerity to ask my parents about. But it was fast becoming that time of the life cycle where the kids begin to gently assume the role of the parents. Not that my folks were infirm by most standards, but with Dad's increasingly fragile physical condition, it was becoming too much for him and Mom to care for a house. When several months earlier my sisters and I had subtly brought up the notion of perhaps moving to some sort of retirement place, my folks weren't exactly enamored of the idea, which is entirely understandable. I don't even like to admit to being forty, so staring the "Golden Years" in the face must be quite difficult. Probably the only thing more difficult would be trying to convince my folks that the time to sell the family home was upon them, and us.

One of the concerns Mom and Dad had always cited when we'd broached the topic of selling the house was where us "kids" would stay when we came home, if Mom and Dad moved to a small condo or something. In reality, this was a non-issue. Melissa had an extra bedroom at her house, and I was always welcome at the home of my close friend Turk. I would spend a lot of time with him and his wife Ann and their kids anyway when visiting back home, and they'd made it clear I was welcome to stay with them anytime, for as long as I wanted. In fact, I'd actually been snowed in at their house one year. I had gone to their place one afternoon, and we suddenly got hit with one of the worst blizzards on record. The roads were completely shut down for about three days, and there was no way I could make it back to Mom and Dad's, even though it was only a couple miles away. Fortunately, Ann had been food shopping the day before, so we were well-stocked. But as the days went by, and we couldn't go anywhere, I suddenly had visions of the movie "Alive" in my head. Ann kept feeding me cookies, and told me she was fattening me up in case they had to eat me to survive. I hoped she was kidding, and silently prayed she wasn't beginning to hallucinate, picturing me as a giant drumstick.

Mom and my sister Melissa were waiting in the car for me. "How was your flight, Eddie?" It always sounded funny to be called "Eddie." The only people who did so were Mom and my sisters. It all started because Dad's name is Ed, and it was easier to call me "Eddie" to avoid confusion in the household. But when I was about ten years old, I expressed to my folks that I was a little bummed that "Eddie" seemed to connote someone not as important as "Ed," so Dad started referring to me as "Big Ed," the name he still called me.

What's in a name? In some instances, plenty. When I was still living in Boston, before moving to LA to write for "Dennis Miller Live," friends in California sent me some clippings about an actor by the name of "Eddie Driscoll." I always thought it was kind of cool to see that in print. When I moved to the west coast, I would occasionally get phone calls for the "other" Eddie Driscoll, and I assumed he was getting some intended for me. I vowed that I'd have to meet him someday.

That day came sooner than I thought when I began to do television and movie appearances and went to sign up to become a member of the Screen Actors Guild. Imagine my shock when the humorless clerk told me that I couldn't use the name "Ed Driscoll" as an on-screen credit because there was already an "Eddie Driscoll" in SAG.

"Well, I'm aware of him, but he always goes by 'Eddie,' and I always go by 'Ed,' so that shouldn't matter, right?"

"I don't think you're listening to me," snapped the clerk. "You can't use the name 'Ed Driscoll.' She seemed to be relishing my confusion and discomfort. Probably a frustrated actor herself.

"Listen," I continued. "I'm a comedian and a writer, I'm not really even an actor."

She eyed me for a moment. "I can believe that."

This was truly incredible. I mean, all I wanted to do was use *my name,* it's not like I wanted to register myself as "Robert DeNiro." This was my real name, for God's sake.

"I really don't see what the problem is," I stammered.

By this time, another equally humorless clerk decided to join the fray. He shook his head patronizingly, and adopted a tone as if he were trying to explain quantum physics to a six-year-old. "People cannot share the same name. That's why it's 'Michael J. Fox,' and not just 'Michael Fox.' Somebody was already registered by that name. Do you understand? You'll need to use your FULL name. Can you comprehend that?"

"You're telling me that I have to be known as 'Edward Raymond Driscoll, Jr.? What am I, a Shakespearean actor?"

"Well, the only way you can use 'Ed Driscoll' is if you get written permission from the other 'Eddie Driscoll.' But for now, you'll have to use the full name."

So, I agreed to register under my ridiculously long name. The two clerks were clearly enjoying their little victory. Then, they asked me for my address, and I couldn't resist. "Well, it's 1810, but can I use that number? I mean, do I have to get permission from every person in the world with 1810 as a street address?" As childish as it was, their looks of irritation were my little victory.

Ultimately, I contacted Eddie Driscoll, and he couldn't have been nicer. I told him I'd gotten phone calls congratulating me on my appearances in various stage plays, though I'd never done any, and he told me he'd gotten many calls congratulating him on his Emmy award, though he'd never won one. It was nice that we got to live vicariously through each other. Bizarrely, it turned out that his roommate at the University of Miami, Florida, was a comedian friend of mine who now lived in Boston. Small world, yet we both agreed it was certainly big enough for two Eddie Driscolls. And so, Eddie Driscoll contacted SAG to let them know that it was okay by Eddie Driscoll that Ed Driscoll use the name Ed Driscoll. I'm sure it was an unhappy day for those two already unhappy clerks I'd dealt with.

As Mom drove us towards home, I marveled at the fact that she was still in such robust health. She seemingly always had been. Honestly, I couldn't remember her being sick a day in her life. She's just one of those people who always eats right, plenty of fruits and vegetables, not many sweets, doesn't drink or smoke, etc. And not just because it isn't good for her, but because she actually prefers those things that happen to be healthy. What a blessing for her. I seem to like everything that's bad for a person, including alcohol to the extent that I became an alcoholic. I guess I was just drinking Mom's share as well as my own. Actually, I think I drank *everybody's* mom's share. Happily, I'd been sober for over ten years, which was a good thing for everybody, with the possible exception of the liquor manufacturers.

As we rolled along, I for some reason began reflecting on the fact that I had never really seen Dad and Mom argue, at least, not in a terrible way. They had always seemed so perfect for each other, and it made me wonder if it was some sort of divine intervention that had brought them together.

Their courtship, which was rather typical of their times, led to their rather untypical fifty-seven years of marriage. Edward R. Driscoll, from Ashtabula, Ohio, met Margaret Fanning, from Chicago, at the US Steel offices in the windy city in 1944. He was an engineer, recently discharged from the navy following W.W.II, and she was working as a secretary elsewhere in the same building. They married on June 13, 1945 in Chicago, and relocated at the request of US Steel from Chicago to Birmingham, Michigan, to Cleveland, Ohio, and ultimately to Pittsburgh, PA, where US Steel had its world headquarters. They purchased a red-brick house on Tyris Drive in the South Hills of Pittsburgh in 1960. They had been on Tyris Drive ever since.

We pulled off of Tyris and into the driveway. It was amazing. The house looked almost exactly the same as it always had. It was easy to picture myself as a little kid, tossing a baseball around in the front yard. It was a lot tougher to picture a "For Sale" sign in that very same yard.

After we'd all grabbed a quick bite at the house, Mom, Melissa, and I drove to the hospital to see Dad. When we walked into his room, Dad's face lit up. "Hi, Big Ed." We shook hands, as we always did. Though we unquestionably loved each other, neither of us was comfortable with the hugging thing. "How are you, Dad?"
"I'm doing well."
Dad was always "doing well." He could be sitting there with his hair on fire and would say he was "doing well," because he'd needed a haircut anyway. His natural optimism was a trait that I somehow didn't pick up genetically, though I'd slowly taught myself to be a bit more optimistic about things as I'd gotten older. Come to think of it, maybe Dad did pass some optimism

along to me, in the form of a time-released gene.

"It's always nice to see you, son, but I wish you hadn't come all the way from LA just because of this."

"Dad, I fly in from LA just to go to football games, so I think I can manage to drop in when you're in the hospital." Mom and Melissa laughed in agreement. Melissa said, "You know Keira's coming in from Cleveland today, and Caitlin will be in from Saratoga Springs tomorrow."

"That better not be because of me," said Dad.

"No, not just because of you, Ed," hedged Mom. "You know how everybody likes to come visit in the summer."

That was true enough. Though obviously it was an easier trip for Melissa, who was divorced and lived in Pittsburgh with my two nephews, Seamus and Ronan. And Keira had a two-hour drive from Cleveland, which was not bad at all, so she came back to visit several times a month. My sister Caitlin and her husband Robert lived in upper New York state, and though it wasn't as short a drive as it was for my other sisters, it still was possible to get to Pittsburgh in a matter of hours. Being in LA, I usually only got home once in the summer, and at Christmas time.

Though Dad insisted he was ready to leave the hospital, we wanted to get the doctor's side of it, just for kicks. Mom and I met the doctor in the hallway. "That was a nasty fall he took, Mrs. Driscoll," Doctor Montini began. Mom shook her head in exasperation, and said, "And a fun time was had by all." The doctor looked puzzled, and I laughed. It was an old expression of Mom's that she had gotten from her mother. Whenever something hellish occurred, Grandma, and now Mom, had always said, "And a fun time was had by all." It was funny for many reasons, not the least of which because it was the most cynical, sarcastic thing my mother ever said, at any time. The fact that it was so out of character made it even funnier. Of course, in Mom's gentle delivery, it didn't sound nearly as caustic as it would coming out of most people's mouths.

"I'm sorry, Doctor. I'm just worried about him," Mom explained. He assured us Dad was fine, and that he could indeed go home soon. Luckily for everyone, especially the nurses he was making crazy with his constant demand to leave, Dad was discharged the following morning.

My sister Keira arrived from Cleveland just in time to welcome Dad home. She's a great person, extremely bright and exceptionally kind. Her true love has always been reading and books, and she'd spent time working in publishing in New York City before taking a job as a librarian at Shaker Heights Public Library. We'd always been kindred souls in many regards, enjoying the arts and lively topical debates, and both way too sensitive for our own good. We got in her car and headed to the airport to pick up Caitlin, who was flying in from Saratoga Springs, New York. Keira and I took advantage of our first opportunity to talk without Mom and Dad within earshot.

"I don't know, Eddie, they have to get out of that house. I think Mom is starting to realize that by now, even though Dad is still in denial."

"Can you imagine saying to Dad, 'you're in denial?'" I chuckled. He'd say, 'What the hell does that even mean? What are you, that Six-pack Chopra guy or something?"

Keira laughed. "Yeah, I guess you could say he's in denial about being in denial."

"Well, listen," I continued, "when Caitlin gets here, the four of us kids can get together today at Melissa's house and figure out how we're going to do this. Hey, maybe we can have them declared legally insane, and get them evicted from their own place!" Keira shot me a bemused look. "Just brainstorming," I murmured.

41

Caitlin was waiting for us at the airport, and, as usual, was full of energetic chatter. A tirelessly cheerful person, she ran her own business, a stationary service called "All The Write Stuff," from the home she shared with her husband of twenty five years, Robert. Robert grew up in Saratoga Springs, and met Caitlin when they were both students at the University of Dayton, in Ohio. In spite of my disgust that they did not attend the same school Dad and I did, Ohio State, I had to concede that they are both great people.

Caitlin is easily the most outgoing person in the family, a natural salesperson. I always thought she'd make a great agent. Not so with Melissa, who lets everyone know exactly what she thinks about any given situation. Melissa has a heart of gold and is bright and engaging, but diplomacy is not her strong suit. She'd attended the very first show I performed in Pittsburgh as a professional comic, and afterwards brazenly told the club owner, "Listen, don't screw over my brother. I've heard about how you show biz guys treat people!" Thank God the guy had a sense of humor, or my career could have been over before it even began.

I helped Caitlin load the incredible amount of luggage she was toting into Keira's car, and we drove directly to Melissa's house to have our family meeting. We all agreed that Dad's increasing fragility was becoming too much for Mom to handle on her own. She was becoming more and more his caretaker, and as she approached the age of eighty-one herself, it was getting tougher on her physically as well. What if she got sick? Dad couldn't cook for himself, and though all us kids would continue to help as much as we could, we couldn't give them the type of supervision they were beginning to need.

Getting them to move was going to be a tough sell. After all, we were all extremely attached to that house on Tyris Drive. While it's true that it's the people inside the house that make the home, there was no denying that the structure itself had become more than just bricks and mortar. It was like a third, all-protecting parent, silently listening to our hopes, dreams, fears, and confrontations, never judging, just being there for us through everything.

I'd briefly entertained the thought of buying the house myself since I was secretly planning to move back to Pittsburgh, but I realized things would just feel too weird being in that house all by myself. Besides, in my mind, it would always belong to my folks, especially my mom. The house meant the world to her. She cooked and cleaned and dusted constantly, like June Cleaver on amphetamines. Over the years she'd applied new carpeting and fresh paint, even though the house was always immaculate anyway without those upgrades. In the last few months, we'd finally convinced her to have a cleaning woman come every other week. But Mom couldn't help herself: she cleaned up before the maid came and then re-cleaned after she left. I used to kid her that housekeeping was her hobby, but we both knew that wasn't true. Housekeeping was her profession, and she was a consummate pro. She was a doting, caring mother and housewife whose husband and children were her first priority. Almost an anachronism in today's society.

At Melissa's house, we went around the table in the same fashion we opened our Christmas presents each year, from oldest to youngest, and each of us made our case for how best to handle this impending crisis. Sort of like the UN, but without the threats of armed intervention. (Well, with fewer of those threats, anyway.) When it came to my turn, I said, "Listen, we all know what an ordeal this whole process is going to be for all of us. Mom and Dad have had great lives, but enough is enough. Let's have them put to sleep. I'll call the vet right now." My sisters laughed in spite of themselves. "Oh, come on, Eddie, that's terrible," said Keira, stifling her giggles. "Listen," I continued, "They've had their time, and now it's ours. I'm sick of it." Okay, it wasn't funny anymore, if it ever was to begin with. But I honestly didn't know how else to cope with it.

"Will you talk to them, Eddie?" asked Caitlin. It was strange that though I was the youngest, the older we all got, the more I was expected to be the family leader. I don't know if it's because I'm the male, or what, but it wasn't something I was entirely comfortable with. If we were the Corleones, I think I had always seen myself more as Fredo than Michael. I just wasn't sure I was up to the responsibility of it all, but I had to do my best. "Okay, sure, I'll initiate everything. But you guys need to back me up." Everyone nodded in agreement, and we decided we'd force a discussion sometime that night at the Tyris house.

None of us could shake the sense of dread we felt when we arrived home for dinner. Dad truly seemed to be "doing well," having re-adjusted to being home again. I felt some slight nausea as I realized we'd basically be saying to him, "Hey, enjoying being back home? Well tough, 'cause you have to move."

Mom had made a big pot of her famous chicken soup, and we all chattered as we ate, that is, my sisters and I did the chattering. Mom sat back and listened in bemusement, chiming in occasionally. Dad did what he usually does at the kitchen table: eat. "I don't know how you all get any food in you, all you do is talk!" he'd grumble, trying to appear annoyed, but we all knew he liked us carrying on like we did. It was good background for his meal, a sort of "white noise" side dish.

At one point, Mom said, "Is there something wrong with the soup? Nobody seems to be eating much."
We were all too nervous to eat.
"No, it's great as usual, Mom," I commented.

"They're too busy talking to eat," Dad theorized.

Mom smiled, then said "Well, it sure is nice to have everyone in the house again." My sisters and I exchanged looks. "Yeah, Mom, about the house," I began. Ugh, this was it. There was no turning back. I'd waded in, and I had to start swimming. I paused for what seemed like an eternity, then blurted, "Keira has something she wants to say about it." Keira looked at me in horror, and so I continued. "No, seriously, we're all concerned about Dad's falls, and the upkeep necessary for a house of this size." Mom chuckled, "Since when have you been concerned about the upkeep of this house? I *still* have to clean up after you!"

Dad put down his soup spoon. "Who's 'we'?" he asked.

"Uh, well, me, and Keira, and Melissa, and Caitlin. Plus a couple of strangers I asked at the mall. I just wanted to get as many opinions as possible." This attempt at humor, meant to reduce my own uneasiness if not everyone else's, just hung in the air like a bad odor. Then Dad said, "Well, as much as we don't want to face it, your mother and I realize that we can't continue to stay here. We've been looking at some brochures for "The Friendship Residence," the retirement community just down the block, and we've even talked to our realtor friend Helen, about putting the house on the market."

The stunned silence that ensued was broken when I involuntarily blurted out, "What?! You can't sell our house!!"

****

"My parents are selling the house, man." I looked across the table to gauge Carl's reaction.
"Wow, that's good, isn't it?" he asked.
I shrugged, and looked around the coffee shop. University of Pittsburgh students were everywhere, some tapping on laptops, others hunched over syllabuses and

49

textbooks. One passed by our table and called out "Hello, professor."

"Well, I know he's not talking to me," I laughed.

Carl waved hello, and turned his attention back to me.

"So, do you like being called 'Professor?'" I asked.

"I guess, though I always wonder if they're just being sarcastic," Carl replied.

Carl Kurlander is a funny man, and a great writer. I'd only recently gotten to know him in the past year or so, even though he'd grown up in Pittsburgh, too. Years previously, Carl had moved to LA and written the movie "St. Elmo's Fire." This launched his writing career into the stratosphere, and he was making an incredible income writing for television and movies, and running the show "Head of the Class" for years. But at some point, he'd become disenfranchised with the Hollywood scene. When he met a woman from Pittsburgh, they moved back to Steel Town.

Carl was now teaching writing full-time at the University of Pittsburgh, and writing novels on the side. He was incredibly happy. I was privileged to be a guest speaker in his class on numerous occasions when I was back in Pittsburgh.

"Seriously, aren't you glad your parents are going someplace safer now?" Carl asked.

"Of course, it's just...weird. You know, I just hate change."

"But sometimes change is good, Ed."

"Right, like when you need to feed the parking meter."

"Seriously, you shouldn't be afraid to shake things up sometimes."

Carl had no idea of the major life change I was planning. And that's even though he was the perfect example of what I was trying to do, that is, perhaps find more meaning in my life by coming back home.

"Carl, let me ask you something. Do you feel that since you moved back here, people somehow view you differently?"

"What do you mean?"

"Well, like you somehow failed by coming back here, because you're less in the 'big-time' now. You know, do they view you...sort of with less respect?"

Carl raised an eyebrow as if he was surprised by my question. "Less respect?" he repeated. "Um, no, not really. At least, not that I've noticed. But even if someone did view me that way for some reason, I really wouldn't care. I feel good about myself, and my family is happy here. Truthfully, I don't know think I feel respected no matter where I go!"

I laughed, and we spent a few more minutes shooting the bull about people in Hollywood that we both knew, then we realized we had to wrap things up so Carl wouldn't be late getting home to his wife and daughter. As he and I went our separate ways on Fifth Avenue, my cell rang. It was Ahmos.

"How's it going, Ed?"

"Good. I just had coffee with Carl, he said to say hello. I'm going to be a guest lecturer for his class in a few weeks."

"Well, he's going to be disappointed."

"No, he's not! I'm always a big hit with his classes!"

"No, he's going to be disappointed that you can't do it, at least not for a while. You're doing a ten-week run at the Comedy Store. I just completed the deal."

Wow, this was cool. The Comedy Store on Sunset Boulevard is the legendary nightclub that has been, and continues to be, home to some of the best comedians in history, including the likes of David Letterman, Jay Leno, Sam Kinison, Chris Rock, etc. I had recently performed there with my friend and comic great Louie Anderson, and management had liked what I was doing and was eager to have my show for ten Saturday nights over the course of the next few months, starting the third week of August. I was elated.

"Good job, Ahmos, even though I think you're making it up just to keep me from moving back here," I kidded.

"Hey, everything out here is falling into its rightful place," Ahmos remarked.

I told him I'd be grabbing a plane back to LA in just a few days. Dad was feeling much better, the house issue was now a non-issue due to Dad's surprise announcement, and the run at the Comedy Store was to begin in just a few days.

CHAPTER TWO

I'd been back in LA for a few days
when I got home in the late afternoon from
a rewrite of a script for Paramount and
found a message on my machine from Tom
Kikta, an old schoolmate from my alma
mater Upper St. Clair High School, or "USC"
as the cool kids called it. Robert was a very
successful musician and teacher of music at
Duquesne University in Pittsburgh. He
informed me that I'd been elected to the
USC Hall Of Fame. I was totally surprised,
mostly because I didn't even know there
was a USC Hall of Fame. Apparently, it had
just been created, and they were honoring
people from the arts, academics, and
athletics. Robert didn't mention which
category I was being honored in, so I used
the process of elimination. My chances for
the academic wing probably went out the
window when I flunked geometry my
sophomore year, and my chances for the
athletic wing disappeared oh, whenever I

tried to do something athletic. So, I guess that left the arts. Cool enough.

All joking aside, I really was honored. I loved my time at USC, and was grateful for the many teachers and fellow students who'd encouraged my sense of humor. I was excited that I had another chance to go back to Pittsburgh, as there would be a ceremony in a few weeks at the school.

The next message on my machine was from Mom. She was calling to tell me that they had sold the house! Wow, they'd put it on the market the day I'd left, and in less than a week it had been sold for its full asking price. They had already put down money on an apartment at "The Friendship Residence." For two people in their eighties, I mused, they seemed to be moving pretty fast. Though it's what my sisters and I had wanted all along, oddly the sale of the house felt like a defeat. In reality, it was probably the difficulty of acknowledging the fleeting passage of time. As much as I tried not to think about it, there was no denying that if my parents were getting older, so was I.

I looked at the clock, and realized it was still early enough back east to call my folks. As I dialed their number, I realized that soon this number would no longer be applicable to my life. It was a phone number that had become a source of comfort in itself. Because for forty years, no matter where I was living, or where I was touring on the road, it was a way for people to get a message to me, or anybody else in our family. Once, a friend from college who I hadn't heard from in fifteen years and was now living in Australia, had seen me win an Emmy on TV. He'd looked up the last number he'd had for me, and left a congratulatory message with my parents. I think my folks were more impressed by the fact I had a friend call from Australia than by the Emmy itself.

I always called my parents at least once a week, usually on Sunday, and more

often if something important was going on, such as
an Ohio State football game. Dad and I are rabid fans, and we'd talk before the game, then at halftime to analyze the action thus far, then at the end to either revel in the victory or bitch about the defeat.

Over the last few years, I'd found myself calling Mom and Dad more and more, because, well, I missed them for one thing, but also because I knew they weren't going to be around forever.

I thought about how when I'd first moved out of their house and got my own apartment in Pittsburgh, then moved to Boston, I'd hardly ever called them. They'd call me, saying, "Hey, just let us know how you're doing," and I was actually annoyed by that. Here I was trying to prove to them that I was "grown up," so much so that I didn't need to call my parents. Little did I realize at the time just how immature that really was, and that calling them on a regular basis as I did now was one of the most "grown-up" things I could ever do.

When I reached Mom and told her about the USC Hall of Fame thing, she was very happy, but she didn't quite sound like herself. I asked what was wrong.

"Oh, I don't know, dear, I've just been feeling a bit sick to my stomach the last few days. Probably all the stress of having to move."

That was certainly understandable. I was half her age when I moved into my house, and it had been stressful beyond belief. I told her to try and take it easy. Melissa got on the phone, and said that everything was rolling along smoothly. The movers had been booked, and the folks were going to leave the house and move into Friendship Residence in mid-September.

I realized that that schedule would work out perfectly for me as well. I was supposed to come back to be inducted into USC in September, so I'd just take some time to help clean out the Tyris house. I'd return to LA, then go back to Pittsburgh again a few days later to help get my parents situated in their new home.

Dad got on the phone, and tried to reassure me that they didn't need my help. "Between the movers and myself, we've got it covered." Great, just what I wanted to picture, Dad trying to move a bunch of the stuff himself. "Well, I have to come in for the high school thing anyway, Dad, so can't I stick around?"

"Well, of course. It's always good to see you. That's a nice thing they're doing for you at the school."

"It's about time they honor me!" I kidded.

"I thought they honored you pretty well when they made you sweep up the halls after you got caught throwing snowballs at that school bus."

Hmm, I always wondered where I'd inherited my smart-ass attitude.

I sat backstage at the Comedy Store, supposedly perusing my notes for the show I was about to perform, but I wasn't really focusing on the papers in front of me. I was distracted by all the changes in my life and the lives of those around me. Though I should have been excited to do the first show, I was lamenting the fact that this run would be further delaying my move back east. I couldn't stop ruminating about how strange it was going to be to not have that house on Tyris anymore.

Ahmos came back backstage and asked, "So, are you ready? It's a full house out there."

"Oh, man, don't say 'house' " I muttered.

"What?"

"Nothing. Yeah, I'm ready. When are they introducing me?"

Before Ahmos could answer, we heard the crackle of the PA system, and the words "Ladies and Gentlemen, Ed Driscoll!"

"I think any time now," Ahmos deadpanned.

I bolted out onto the stage in a bit of a panic. Shit, I hated getting surprised by my own introduction!

Oh well, it was the first week, so there was certain to be plenty of kinks to work out.

"Good evening, thanks so much for coming," I said to the crowd as I pulled the microphone from the stand. "I'll be working here at the Store a lot over the next few months. Mostly as a bartender. This will be the only night where I'll actually be permitted to perform." The audience laughed, and I felt myself relax, for what seemed like the first time in quite awhile.

Over the next hour, most of the material hit its mark. But inevitably, some of it thudded with the subtlety of a warhead, a "not-so-smart" bomb. There was work to be done, but I knew that would be the case. A good deal of the material had not been tested in front of an audience before.

To add to the stress, there were the inevitable technical glitches that come with the first performance of any show. At one point, there was a problem with the electricity, and the overhead lights dimmed noticeably right in the middle of a punchline. "Someone must be using their hairdryer," I ad-libbed. I didn't mind the interruption that much since I at least got a laugh out of it. But when it happened again minutes later, I started getting irritated. "What are they doing, executing people?" I asked as the lights flickered yet again. "If so, maybe they should start with the guy in charge of lighting." (It's one of the great things about comedy, you can make all kinds of sarcastic, insulting remarks under the guise of merely doing your job.)

Despite the unintended strobe effect of the Comedy Store's lighting, the show went well, and I left the stage to thunderous applause. I felt great, and was already looking forward to my next performance. Ahmos greeted me backstage with a high-five, and several people from my agency made their way back into the green room. Everyone seemed very pleased.

"Wow, you were really funny, Ed!"
exclaimed one agent.

"Well, gosh, don't sound so surprised!" I
answered.

As various people connected with the
production mingled and snacked on the
ever-present backstage deli platters, Ahmos
and I quietly huddled and began talking
about what had worked and what hadn't,
and made plans to review the videotape of
the show. That was the one part of the job
I dreaded most. I hate watching myself,
because my mind goes right to the
negatives I perceive about myself, often
personal negatives that have nothing to do
with the professional negatives I am
supposed to be critiquing. I don't like how I
look, how I sound, etc. Not to mention how
uncomfortable it is watching the jokes that
didn't work. But as painful as the process is,
reviewing tape is one of the best ways to
improve, so I always did my best to put
aside my personal discomfort. As in life, it's

necessary to examine oneself closely in order to grow. Often, to relieve the tension while viewing the tape, I'll viciously heckle my image out loud, just to make Ahmos laugh and myself feel less sheepish. We agreed to meet at Ahmos' office the following day to review the video.

I was pretty wound up when I got back home that night, as I usually am after a performance, especially one that has gone well. I was full of adrenaline-fueled energy. It was similar in nature to a sugar rush, an intense burst of energy that would peak, then suddenly deplete, leaving me vaguely unsettled, and often exhausted. Back in the day, I used to handle it by ingesting ridiculous amounts of booze, but that option had been off the table for some time now. I found that pulling out one of my chess books and replaying a classic game from the past often enabled me to focus that extra energy. Yep, a typical Hollywood story. Entertainer all jacked up on applause, then heads back to his swinging bachelor pad and tragically overdoses on Fischer-Spassky.

I looked at the wide variety of chess sets on display in my living room. Many, if not most, were gifts from friends. I had fun, silly ones like "The Simpsons," given to me by friends that write on that show, and a "Red Sox vs. Yankees" set from my BoSox fan brother-in law, Robert. There were many esthetically classic sets, too, such as the one Ahmos had brought me back from a trip to Egypt, and a gorgeous hand-carved table and set I'd purchased myself from a store in New York City.

It was good to be in my home enjoying my surroundings, though my house certainly seemed a bit empty now that I was living there by myself. After my engagement with Rita had broken up, I'd dated a woman named Heather who, because of circumstances with her own apartment, ended up moving in with me. It soon turned out that she had a fear of commitment not even she had been aware of, but had reared its ugly head once we were cohabitating, and she felt she had to deal with it alone. I had to respect that, especially since it would be hard for me to ever believe her in the future if she eventually announced that she was ready to get married. Though I wasn't even thinking about marriage at that point, I would have wanted that option to be on the table in the future.

At one point, she offered to just stay together as friends and lovers, without the "piece of paper." But I ended up surprising her, and myself, when I told her that I wanted a wife, and a family, and that my "shacking up" days were behind me. When I found myself saying to her, "Well, if we can't take this to the next level, there's no reason to be together," I wondered what was wrong with me! I was basically saying, "Listen, if you think you're gonna stay here and have sex with me without demanding a commitment, well, you've got another thing coming, missy! What kind of a guy do you think I am?"

It certainly seemed to be a gender reversal of the stereotypical 'woman wants commitment, guy avoids commitment' dynamic. I was actually freaked out by my steadfast insistence on that "piece of paper," so much so that I called my shrink about it. She told me my new attitude was merely a case of "maturity." Obviously, that wasn't something I'd been accused of very often. As sad as it all was, we parted as great friends. (Heather and I, that is. I assume my shrink and I are together for life!) While I was fairly certain I'd done the right thing, the loneliness sometimes whispered to me that perhaps I hadn't.

****

Keira, Caitlin, Melissa, and I gathered around the kitchen table at the Tyris house and attempted to plan a strategy to get things ready for our parents' impending move. With Mom on the job, the place had always been clean, but now it had to be thoroughly cleared out from top to bottom. Living in a place for forty years, clutter tends to form as if by its own volition. Caitlin and I agreed to work on the attic, and I climbed the rickety ladder that led to the top of the house. As I reached the highest rung, I flipped on the light and was incredulous at the sheer volume of items. I pondered that it would be a lot simpler to just set fire to the entire structure than to sort and remove all of this stuff. But, not wanting to accidentally torch something truly valuable like comic books or GI Joes, I used the more conventional method of picking through the clutter piece by piece.

There was some really nifty stuff up there. I found my old electric football game, and as I picked up the box, the little plastic players spilled out everywhere. Hey, the Colts versus the Packers! I remembered as a kid taking hours to set up each side, then flipping the switch to watch the little men do nothing but spin in circles. It was just like real football! At least, it seemed so when I was ten.

I found a bunch of my old 'Hot Wheels' cars. Just like when I was a little kid, I eagerly assembled the pieces of orange plastic track that the cars rode on. I realized that this is what they needed for *real* cars, large orange track with side rails to keep people in their lanes. The roads in LA would be much safer if we could get the state highway department to build freeways with the same care that the folks at Mattel did.

As I continued the attic excavation, I stumbled upon my first chess set. Like thousands of other Americans, I'd gotten the chess bug back when Bobby Fischer put the game on the front pages of all the newspapers with his match for the world title against Boris Spassky in 1972. I was eleven years old, and Greg, my next-door neighbor and old man of fourteen, taught me how to play. We'd have furiously competitive games, often marked by someone hurling their King across the room at the end of the contest. I once accidentally hit Greg above the eye with my knight, causing a welt that lasted for weeks. Only in Pittsburgh would chess be a contact sport. I actually got pretty good at it, and won my grade school championship. But as I got to high school and college, my interests were pulled in many other directions, and I'd put the game down for about ten years. But when I caught mononucleosis in the late 1980's, Mom bought me a hand-held chess playing computer to fill my time while I recovered, and my interest in the game was renewed. I'd played very steadily, at home against computers as well as against humans, and in tournaments, ever since.

As I made my way through the boxes, Caitlin and Melissa decided to help, which in theory should have made it all go faster, but in fact seemed to have the opposite effect. As we hauled the boxes filled with photos and souvenirs and old clothes down into the master bedroom, my sisters couldn't resist going through every item in painstaking detail. The sheer volume of items continued to amaze us all. It seemed like the only thing missing from that attic was Anne Frank. I had no idea my folks were such pack rats. This stuff probably should have been cleared out long ago.

Interestingly, Mom was the least sentimental of anyone, at least on the surface. Every time she encouraged me to throw something out, one of my sisters would protest. "Mom, you can't throw that out, it's your old high school pin!" Mom could see where all this was going, and she was having none of it. "Well, dear, you can have it, but make sure you store it at *your* house and not this one!"

At one point while I was picking my way through the far corner of the attic, I came upon a dead bird, a sparrow. It showed absolutely no signs of injury or decay, and if I hadn't known better, I'd have sworn it was merely napping. It lay on its side with what could only be described as a peaceful look on its face. For some reason, I was mesmerized. Normally, I'd have done the mature thing; picked the bird up and chased my sisters around with it. But I couldn't do anything. I just stared at it for what felt like hours. Finally, I gingerly lifted it up and took it outside. I dug a little hole in the ground near our garden, and somberly buried the peaceful-looking creature.

We took a break for dinner, then Mom and the girls worked on the dishes, while I helped Dad sort through some of the stuff he'd been accumulating in the garage. I shuddered when I saw the spot where he'd fallen trying to replace that bulb.
"You know, Dad, it'll be a good thing for you guys not to have to deal with all these chores."

"Yeah, I know. But it's sort of hard to face that, you know?"

I nodded, and we continued laboring in silence.

We worked our way through various paint cans that had stacked up over the years. Dad must have never thrown out any paint in his life. There were colors from his original house in Chicago. Hell, I think some of Leonardo DaVinci's touch-up paint was in there, too.

Dad was giving a lot of the paint away to various neighbors, who I guessed would store it in their garages until they themselves had to move. I don't think the paint is ever actually used; it's just passed from generation to generation like season tickets. Dad knew there was no use in giving it to me. I'd never developed his passion to be a "do it yourself-er." I was more of a "I'll gladly pay you to do it for me-er." Dad and I shared a passion for sports, as well as a dry sense of humor, but were so different in so many other ways.

He's very logical, being a metallurgical engineer. Of course, children often rebel against their folks, and I was no exception. I rebelled by sucking at science and math. I was somehow drawn to the arts, finding language and history much more palatable.

As we went through some more boxes, we were reminded of a funny incident involving the family beagle, Breezy, who had since passed on and presumably was drinking from that giant toilet bowl in the sky. When she was a puppy, we were paper-training her, and she was learning to relieve herself on the newspapers we put on the floor. One day Dad was working underneath our car, and put down newspapers to lay on so he wouldn't get dirty. As we were looking around his workbench for a specific tool he needed, Breezy wandered into the garage, spotted the newspapers, and did what she was supposed to do. We were pretty surprised to walk into the garage and see Breezy squatting underneath the car. We couldn't stop laughing, and Breezy seemed slightly confused, yet pleased that she was obviously bringing us so much joy.

After several hours, we decided to call it a night. Everyone in the family was pretty drained, physically and emotionally, and we all headed upstairs to go to sleep. Melissa stayed in her house a couple miles away, with her sons, but the rest of us stayed at the folks.' I slept in my old room at the end of the hall, and Keira in hers next to my parents. Caitlin bunked down in her old room, the one she used to share with Melissa.

The house was quiet, at least, for awhile. Then, the air was shattered by the sounds of Dad's buzz saw-like snoring. I'd forgotten how loud he could get. I don't know how Mom ever slept through it. I guess it's a matter of getting used to it. After all, as a kid I always heard it, but it didn't really keep me awake. However, it was keeping me awake this night, so I finally got up and went back downstairs. I fired up the TV and put on "SportsCenter."

I reflected on the many times I had sat up by myself as a teenager, watching sports on late night TV when everyone else had gone to bed. Quite often, I'd go into my parents' liquor cabinet, and pour myself a glass, or two, or ten, of whiskey or vodka. Then, I'd carefully fill the bottle back to its previous level with tap water, so that my parents wouldn't notice any was missing.

In reality, it was very unlikely that they'd notice, because they weren't really 'drinkers,' at least, not in the stereotypical Irish family way. Mom almost never drank, except maybe half a glass of wine at Christmas. And Dad would drink a beer each evening before dinner, and that was it. The only time they really used anything in the liquor cabinet is when they hosted a party. My poor folks, I always imagined them serving this stuff to their friends, not knowing how much I'd diluted it all. I pictured our neighbors saying to each other quietly, "The Driscolls are nice people, but it's odd that they water down their liquor." Thanks to me, my parents were unwittingly serving the weakest drinks in town.

Fortunately, I was no longer compelled to engage in that type of destructive behavior, having been part of a twelve-step program since my days in Boston. I was more than content with a tall glass of milk as I watched the baseball highlights.

The next morning, we sat around the breakfast table, planning our chores for the day. "Hey, Dad, were you doing some woodworking in your room last night?" I needled. Mom laughed. "I guess you haven't heard that in awhile, huh Eddie?" I retorted, "Actually, Mom, I can hear Dad's snoring all the way out in California. People out there just think it's another earthquake."

I was due at the high school that afternoon for the hall of fame induction. I gave my sisters good-natured grief that they couldn't attend the ceremony. Unfortunately, neither Dad nor Mom was feeling very well, and though they wanted to attend, I insisted that they didn't. Mom's stomach was really bothering her, and Dad's most recent fall had left him more fragile than ever. I assured them I'd tell them all about it, and come see them as soon as the festivities were over.

I strode up the sidewalk leading to the front door of Upper St. Clair High. There was a hand-painted banner hanging over the entrance reading 'Welcome, Hall of Fame Inductees.' I remembered making plenty of those very type of banners when I was in high school. It was a mainstay of after-school activities. In twelfth grade, I had been elected a "Senior Senator." I was in charge of representing the senior class's interests at council meetings. Truthfully, for me it was an excuse to avoid real work, pad my resume, and further my own interests. In other words, just like being an actual U.S. Senator. And whenever there was a function at the school, us kids involved in student government were in charge of the advertising. It was a great chance to mix with the girls, and of course, with the teenage years being such a festival of hormones, it was somehow fairly erotic watching them smearing that paint around. Of course, at sixteen, *everything* was somehow fairly erotic. Heck, I'd get erections when the school bus ride was extra bumpy.

My favorite challenge back then was trying to come up with a slogan for whatever the particular occasion was, a slogan that was funny without being too vulgar. After all, these signs had to be approved by the faculty and some of our favorites never made it past the design stage. Such as the dinner held to honor teacher Mrs. Fiok, when we made a large banner reading, "Congratulations, and Fiok

You." Or during football season, "Come to the Poop Rally, and support our Crappy team." Sadly, I think my sense of humor hasn't really matured much since then.

I was greeted at the door by the principal of the school, Dr. William Pope. He'd been in the system at USC forever, and was due to retire that next year. When I saw him, I feigned surprise and horror and blurted, "Oh man, it's Pope. I'm busted!" He laughed and we shook hands. He was always a nice man, and I was glad to see him. He congratulated me on my success, and said he was so happy that I'd come back from LA for the ceremony. I told him I was only there to make up a gym class I'd skipped in 1979.

Dr. Pope, just like most of my teachers, had always been so incredibly supportive. Of course, as there always seems to be in life, there were a few naysayers back then. One person *not* at the event was a former teacher who used to always say to me in disgust, "Hey, Driscoll!

There's ten thousand unemployed comedians out there, and you're trying to break into the business." I wasn't sure where he was now, the last I'd heard he was unemployed.

A young man named Ernie, a member of the current student government, was on hand to give me a tour of the school. USC High had changed immensely in my twenty years away. It had almost doubled in size, with the addition of new classrooms and labs, and a new gymnasium. This growth merely reflected the steady increase in population of the area over the last decade. People were discovering, or perhaps re-discovering, that it was a great place to live. The campus itself was beautiful, and I was really impressed with the design of the architecture. I smiled to myself as I remembered just how many great fun and educational moments I'd had at USC, and how much I'd grown there as a young man, often in spite of myself.

"So, Ernie," I whispered, "you seem to be 'the man' around here, does that mean you can score me some hookers?" He looked shocked, then burst out laughing. "I'm kidding, of course," I added quickly. Geez, what the hell was I doing making a joke like that to a kid?, I admonished myself. Twenty years out of high school, and I was still trying to show other kids that I was "cool."

As we were wrapping up our little tour, Tom Kikta arrived. "Thanks for basically throwing away your standing in the community by nominating me, Robert," I told him as we shook hands. We reminisced about a show we'd done together when we were seniors at USC. We'd been drafted to entertain at the St. Thomas Moore summer cookout, and the way my stand-up went over, I felt like the one who'd ended up burnt. Robert had played his guitar, and was much better received than my humor. "You were really good, even back then, Ed, it wasn't your fault. It was a bad crowd," said

Robert. "Yeah, but unfortunately, that was the best I've ever done to this day!" I lamented. Robert laughed, and continued, "It's so great that you had the courage to leave Pittsburgh to follow your dreams. Nobody wins Emmys back here!" Before I could respond, we were interrupted by young Ernie. "Mr. Driscoll, they're ready to begin the ceremony now. Can I take you to your seat?"

Jim Bennett, a man who'd been a driving force in the arts at USC way before I'd been there and ever since I left, presented me with a statue signifying my induction. It was surprisingly beautiful. For some reason, I was expecting something made by a freshman in shop class as part of his detention assignment. I wondered to myself if the kids were still carving out bongs in woodworking class.

As I mingled following the ceremony, I came upon many teachers who by now had retired, but there were also quite a few that were still working there, which boggled my mind. I was happy to spot my old social studies teacher, and I made my way across the crowded floor to greet him.

"Hi, Mr. Pearce," I said, suddenly sounding as though I was fifteen again.

"Ed, I think you can call me 'Al' at this point."

I laughed. "I'm not sure I can, it doesn't feel quite right, but I'll try...Al."

We chatted a bit about how much the school had grown over the years, and Mr. Pearce, I mean Al, told me he was retiring this year.

"So, are you thinking of moving somewhere else?" I asked.

He looked puzzled. "Nope."

"Really?" I asked. "Not someplace warmer, a place easier to enjoy retirement?"

Al shook his head. "I never felt the need to live anywhere else when I was working, so I don't feel the need to live anywhere else when I'll just be goofing off."

I nodded. "You know, Al, you and the other teachers I had...it's funny, when you're a kid, even when you like your teachers, you don't really fully appreciate them until later in life. Now that I'm supposedly an adult, I realize how lucky I was to have people like you teaching and supporting me in those formative years."

Al smiled. "Are you setting me up for a joke?" he asked with his eyes twinkling.

"No, not at all. I'm sure you had your fill of my jokes back when I was in your class."

"You were always funny, Ed. Disruptive sometimes, but funny nonetheless."

"Well, thanks, and sorry about the 'disruptive' part. And hey, I'm sorry I never said 'thanks' for all you did back then, but I certainly want to say it now. Thanks."

"You might find this hard to believe, Ed, but it was truly my pleasure." Al's smile was more rewarding than receiving the hall of fame statue itself. But since I wasn't comfortable asking Al to sit on my mantle, I settled for the statue.

After the event was over, I drove back to see Mom and Dad. They were looking pretty tired, understandably so, yet their eyes brightened when I brought them my statue. I told them I'd like to give it to them as a housewarming present for when they move into the new place, being that I was too cheap to actually buy them something.

"So, Eddie, how did everything go? Did you have fun?" asked Mom. "Well," I offered, "Nobody asked me to the Sadie Hawkins dance, so I can't help but feel a bit disrespected." Mom and Dad laughed, and I continued.

"It was really a nicely done affair. Great food, super nice people...the only thing missing was my parents. But again, I think it's smart that you guys stayed home. You both need to recover your health."

"We'll be there next time, dear," assured Mom.

The next morning, Helen, the realtor who was selling the house for my parents, stopped by to talk things over with all of us. I wanted to be part of the discussion before I caught my plane back to LA that night. Helen remarked on the excellent shape the Tyris house was in. "I imagine the house has a lot of sentimental value to you all," she said. "Oh, yes," said Keira. "I mean, goodness, Breezy is buried in the back yard!" I turned to Helen and said, "Breezy was our maid." She looked at me for a moment, then everyone burst out laughing. Helen said, "I see you're working on your act, Ed." In my mind, I wished I *was* working on my act. That comedy stuff was relatively easy for me. Real life stuff, that's what I found so challenging.

Finally, it was time for me to head to the airport. I kissed Mom goodbye, and shook hands with Dad. I told them I planned to come back shortly to help with the move to the retirement home, and would continue to come back as often as I could to help in whatever way I could. Keira drove me to the airport, and though I normally can't sleep on airplanes, I nodded off the instant I boarded, and slept until the moment we touched down in LA. After all, plane engines weren't nearly as loud as Dad's snoring.

****

I spent my first afternoon back in California at the LA Chess Club. I loved getting lost in those sixty-four squares. I played against my computer a lot at home, but it was always more interesting to play against another human. For one thing, a human will occasionally make mistakes, which computers never do, unless it involves my bank statement. For another thing, I enjoy the camaraderie, and it's fun to discuss the game afterwards with somebody who has the same passion for chess.

One of my favorite opponents was an elderly man named Chester. We were of approximately the same playing strength, so our games were always close and interesting. Chester was in his eighties, and

he liked to joke that he'd once defeated
Benjamin Franklin in a match. I'd always
tease him that the only reason he won was
that Franklin was just a kid when they'd
played. He had been widowed for about ten
years, but his two sons lived nearby, and he
enjoyed spending time with them, and his
grandchildren, and of course, playing chess.

As we sat and played, Chester
mentioned that I seemed distracted.
"Distracted? What are you doing, Chester,
giving me an excuse for games I lose?"
"Well, I knew you'd make up some excuse,
so I figured I'd just make one up for you."
"Thanks. Chester, did you know that Bobby
Fischer was U.S. Champion at age
fourteen?"
"Yes, I did."
"And Kasparov became World Champion at
age twenty-two."
"Yeah, I knew that, too. So?"
I paused. "Well, doesn't that make you
think?"

"Yeah. It makes me think, 'what the hell are you talking about?'"

"Seriously, Chester. I mean, what were you doing at age twenty-two?"

He laughed. "Hell, I don't even remember what I was doing this morning."

I could tell Chester knew exactly what I was getting at, and was just trying to make light of the conversation; but I was on a roll.

"Did you know that Mozart had written all his violin concertos by the time he was twenty? When I was twenty, I was selling my blood plasma to buy used CDs."

Chester seemed nonplussed, so I continued. "By the age of thirty, Thomas Edison had invented the phonograph and the lightbulb. When I was thirty, I was trying to get my stereo to work by banging it with a flashlight. And Beethoven was a massively successful composer by the time he was thirty-eight, though he was deaf! In my late thirties, I learned how to play chopsticks on my nephew's toy piano while nursing an ear infection!"

Chester chuckled. "Well, don't forget, JFK was president at forty-three, Ed. What do you think about that?"

"I think I have a lot of work to do," I exclaimed. "Plus, maybe I should cancel my engagement at the Dallas Comedy Club."

"Ed, why are you so intent on comparing yourself to people from history that you never even knew? And why are you assuming that 'professional success,' whatever that is, leads to having a meaningful life?"

I absent-mindedly pushed my king's bishop pawn two squares ahead. "Then what *is* meaningful? If one's occupation is merely superficial, then all that leaves is a person's personal life."

Chester moved his knight. "Now you're getting dangerously close to making some sense."

I retreated my rook to safety. "But here's the thing; what defines 'personal' success? Certainly, my failed attempt to get married doesn't qualify as a 'success.' I envy the fact my parents have been together for fifty-seven years, and I can't even get a second date."

"How about a second game instead?" asked Chester.

"Let's finish this one first," I muttered.

"Okay then." Chester dropped his queen right next

to my king. "Checkmate."

"You know, you're not helping my esteem with moves like that!" I complained. "Let's try one more game."

As we slowly placed the pieces back on their original squares, Chester fixed me with a look. "Ed, exactly what is it that you're searching for? Meaning, or achievement?"

"I don't quite follow you," I mumbled.

"They're often very different things."

I gave him a puzzled look. "I guess I'm greedy, but I was really hoping for both."

Chester smiled as he adjusted his knights so that both horse heads looked to his right. "Well, I know you're not greedy. The way you care for your folks is not the sign of a greedy person. And the fact that you're moving back to Pittsburgh for them tells me you're not greedy."

"But my move is not only for them. It's also for me."

Chester looked at me warily. "Listen, you want to play another, or not?"

I nodded, and pushed my king's pawn to king four.

✴✴✴✴✴✴✴✴✴✴✴✴

"That's the last box, folks."

The movers had loaded everything into their trucks, and there was nothing left to do now but accept that there was nothing left to do. We'd moved what furniture would fit into my parents' new apartment at the Friendship Residence, and put the rest in the basement of Melissa's home. Of course, I'd shipped my "toys" back to LA, and Caitlin and Keira would be taking certain items back to their places.

It had been quite a day. People from all over the neighborhood had been stopping by all afternoon, somberly presenting homemade cookies, cakes, and pies to our family. It felt sort of like an Irish wake for our house. My folks had been a staple of the neighborhood for forty years, and though they were only moving a few miles away, our friends and neighbors felt a real sense of loss to see them go. And I'm sure at some level it reminded some of them, many of whom were nearing my parents' age, that they too would perhaps need to avail themselves of assisted living in the not-so-distant future.

I had known most of our neighbors since I'd been a child. Though I was purportedly an adult by this time, I still found myself uncomfortable calling them by their first name, so I was always saying, "Hello, Mr. Keener. Hi, Mrs. Keener," sounding like I was Eddie Haskell talking to Beaver's parents.

Despite the somewhat melancholy feelings of the occasion, I was glad to be there, enjoying the collective feeling of a true "neighborhood." This was definitely missing in Los Angeles. Remember Henrietta, my forensic, plant-investigating neighbor? If "Leafgate" had been the only unpleasant episode I'd endured with her, I'd have been happy. But I'd have been awfully surprised, as well. Sure enough, several months after her agronomic detective work, I had yet another bizarre encounter with our neighborhood's own resident malcontent.

Our street allows for public parking, no stickers or permits required, which is a rarity for Los Angeles. It's a definite bargaining chip when trying to convince people to come to my house, whether it's for a personal or professional visit. Every time I invite someone to my house, their very first question is always, "How's the parking there?" My proud answer: "Free and plentiful." People are excited that they can actually find a place to park in LA without worrying about being ticketed, towed, or broken into. Well, two out of three isn't bad. Anyway, I usually park directly in front of my own house, but one evening I came home and the only spaces available were in front of Darth Neighbor's house. In fact, there were three available spaces there, so I parked and went inside for the evening.

As I walked to my car the following morning, I noticed something fluttering beneath my windshield wiper. "Nuts," I thought to myself, "Is this a street cleaning day? How did I get a ticket?" As I got closer, I noticed it wasn't a ticket, but rather some kind of note. As it turned out, it wasn't just a note, it was an entire symphony of insanity. It was a long, multi-page, hand-written tirade from Henrietta, informing me that only she and her "guests" were permitted to park in front of her house. *"You need to respect my house,"* she wrote at one point. Wow, I didn't realize what an insult it was to park my Lexus in front of her property. What a blow that must have been to her reputation. How could I have been so thoughtless? Of course, she had often parked the smoldering pile of metal that she called a car in front of my place. But I guess that was a sign of *respect* for my house.

"What if it was trash day, and I had to put my barrels in the street?" her note demanded. Hmm, good point. I guess she'd have to somehow squeeze the tiny barrels into the twenty feet of clear space on either side of my car.

"I've lived here since 1955, so I think I know what it means to be a good neighbor." I guess she does, and it was good of her to educate me. Apparently, "good neighbors" approach other neighbors' legally parked vehicles and leave rambling, incoherent scribblings that Charles Manson would look at and say, "Wow, this shit's crazy."

I think the capper of it all was the stationary itself. She'd taken the time to scrawl a rude, bile-filled manifesto on cute little paper that featured bear cubs playing with jars of honey. How precious! Perhaps I could give her a note saying, "Fuck You!" jotted in an adorable little "Garfield" card.

As I was still reading this newly minted companion piece to "Mein Kampf," Henrietta suddenly came barging out her front door. She was attired in a bright red housecoat, looking for all the world like a runaway barn.

"Do not park there!" she shouted, flailing her arms around as if she was being attacked by bees. She looked as though she was going to have a heart attack. Of course, she'd have probably died because surely when the ambulance arrived, she wouldn't have let the medics park in front of her house.

I was pretty aggravated myself at this point, but I kept my cool. "Listen, Henrietta," I began, "I didn't park here in order to insult you. This is a public street, and it's not reasonable to leave nasty notes on people's cars like this."

"YOU GO TO HELL!!" she screamed at me. Well, this was just sad. Clearly she was a sick woman, and it wouldn't be nice to say something angry to a person who was obviously mentally ill.

"I don't tell you where to park your broom, you psychotic witch!" I shouted back. Okay, it wasn't nice, but it actually felt pretty good.

She stopped in her tracks, put her hands on her hips, shook her head at me, then stormed back inside her house. I calmly got into my car and drove away, feeling as though I'd just survived a run-in with a wild boar.

When I came back later that afternoon, thankfully there was space in front of my own house, so I parked there. But when I got out of my car, I saw that Henrietta was in her front yard, berating some poor guy who'd had the misfortune to park in front of the Ayatollah's palace. I actually felt disappointed. Here it turns out she yells at *everyone*, and suddenly I just didn't feel quite as special.

My parents had said their last goodbyes to their neighbors, and it was time to make our way to the Friendship Residence. It was a really lovely facility, which was fortunate considering the somewhat sad circumstances under which people generally arrived there. It included its own laundry service, spa, and library. It had only been open for about a year, and everything was still sparkling new. Rather than resembling a medical facility, it felt more like a luxury hotel, albeit one with unusually fragile guests. Thus, I dubbed the residence "The Broken Arms" hotel, to my parents' amusement.

Mom got busy right away decorating the apartment, putting up pictures, and telling us where to put all the furniture. "Gosh, Mom, what did you do before you had us kids?" I asked as I strained to move the couch for the fifth time. "She made *me* do it all," Dad chimed in. I knew he was saying that to be funny, but there was a certain sadness to the comment. He had indeed done it all, and enjoyed doing it. And now he couldn't do much anymore.

Mom got out my USC Hall of Fame statue, and proudly put it up on the little mantle in their little living room, as my sisters mocked me. Mom was doing her best to keep a brave face, but she was obviously feeling the strain of everything. She admitted to me privately that she was glad they were doing this for Dad's sake, but that she's always loved having a house, and that she'd miss it. I tried to emphasize the fact that it would be a lot more relaxing for her to not have to worry about the constant upkeep of a house. Plus, they were still living quite close to their friends, and they'd certainly meet new ones here.

"I don't know, Eddie, I don't mean to be judgmental, but it's just a little depressing to be around so many people as old as me."

"But Mom, look at the staff, and the families that I'm sure constantly visit. There seem to be people of all ages hanging around, from what I can tell. It's going to be fine, Mom, it really is."

I understood her concern, and was trying my hardest to conceal the fact that I shared it, too.

Melissa left to pick up my nephews from school to bring them over to Mom and Dad's new place. We all went to dinner together right there at the Residence. The dining hall was incredible. A burly, friendly guy ambled out of the kitchen and introduced himself as Deke, the head chef. It turned out that Deke was quite accomplished, having come over from one of the leading restaurants in town. His culinary abilities were so good that the dining facility was actually open to the public on Sundays for brunch. Lots of families would come to visit their relatives, and lots of people from the neighborhood who had no family residing there still came to enjoy Deke's mixing bowl artistry.

After dinner, we went back to the apartment to talk for a bit. Mom expressed her dismay that there wasn't room for us to stay with them now, but we assured her we wouldn't be sleeping in an alley. Caitlin had to go back to Saratoga the next day, and Keira was leaving for Cleveland that evening, so that she could be at work in the morning. I was going to stay with Turk and his family. Mom walked all us kids to the door, and we said good-bye.

As we made our way to our cars, Melissa pulled me aside to tell me that while Mom's stomach was still bothering her, she'd shown some good signs of being her old self. When Melissa had arrived with the kids for dinner, she found Mom already "helping" the staff at the Residence by showing them how they could better clean some of the many artifacts that were on display in the building. Melissa told me Mom was going to the doctor on Monday just to make sure everything was okay. As for Dad, he seemed to be doing well, and in fact, when we left he was seen checking out their neighbor's deluxe walker, one of those models with wheels and a basket on the front, and showing genuine interest in acquiring one himself.

It was all a strange feeling, and I thought it must be akin in a way to what Mom and Dad had felt when they'd dropped us kids off at kindergarten for the first time. There's something unnerving about knowing that no matter what, from that point on, things were never going to be quite the same.

★★★★★★★★★★★

"Seriously, what is the problem with the fucking lights?" I'd gone from being funny about it to unbridled rage. The audience shifted in their seats uncomfortably. This Comedy Store show wasn't going as well as the previous ones. The crowd was smaller, and less giving, and I was distracted. It wasn't their fault, and I knew it, but when the lights flickered this time, I couldn't stop myself from losing my temper.

Earlier that day, Melissa had called to tell me that Dad had fallen again. Fortunately, there was medical assistance available immediately because of where they now lived, but he was banged up pretty bad. Mom was pretty freaked, but at least Dad was actually using his cane now, and seemed to finally realize he needed it.

The uneasiness of the situation stuck with me all day, and I started feeling resentful that I was in LA when all this happened. When I got to the club that night to do my show, the anxiety joined me as I took the stage. But snapping publicly about the lights jolted me back into a state of professionalism, and I realized I had to concentrate on entertaining these people who'd come to see me. I was able to extricate myself from the tension of the moment by making some jokes about everybody bringing their own flashlights to the show next time, in lieu of actual stage lighting. The audience could sense I was relaxing, which made them relax, which in turn made it easier for me to relax. Amazing how we were all intertwined together in this thing.

The show finished on an up note, but backstage I was disgusted at myself for not doing as well as I could have. "I hope nobody from my high school was here, they might pull me out of the hall of fame," I ruefully said to Ahmos.

I promised myself that for my next show I'd keep my cool no matter what, and give the people who paid to see me the best possible show I could. Some people think performers are indifferent to the audience, because many entertainers purposely try to give that impression. But it's my contention that that's just whistling past the graveyard. Every performer wants his audience to be satisfied, even if it sometimes appears otherwise, and I was determined to let none of my outside issues impose themselves on my work like that again.

The next morning, I was eating breakfast when my phone rang. The caller ID read "Friendship Residence." I figured I'd freak out Mom by answering, "Hi Mom. What's up?"

"How did you know it was me?"

"I have supernatural powers, Mom. I got them from you."

"You mean like a sixth sense?"

"Yes. But it's actually called 'Caller ID.' What's going on, Mom?"

There was a several second pause, and I instantly felt sick. Something was definitely wrong.

"Well, honey, I'm afraid I've got some bad news from the doctor," she said, her voice shaking slightly.

"Oh, no. What's happened to Dad now?"

"He's fine, dear. But...I have cancer."
I felt my knees turn to Jell-O and I sat down. This wasn't happening. Hopefully, the alarm on my nightstand would go off any second now, and I'd find I was just having a bad dream.
"What do you mean?" I asked incredulously.
"You know I haven't been feeling very well, and I went to the doctor. He said it probably was just nerves from the move and all, but they took some tests to be certain. And they found cancer on my ovaries."

How in the world could this be? Every night on the news, I had to hear how Osama Bin Laden, a man who seemingly existed for the sole purpose of murdering people, was somehow surviving bombs and bullets and a reported kidney condition. But my mom, who's never been anything but kind and loving to every person she's ever met, has fucking cancer?
"What's the next step, Mom?"

"They want to start chemotherapy on me right away. They think they might have found it in time."

"I'm sure they have, Mom. I'm sure of it. It's going to be okay, you'll see."

Dad got on the phone very briefly, and was trying to sound tough, but he was clearly struggling to keep from crying. I told them I was coming back home. They tried to dissuade me, saying I had to pay attention to my work. Yeah, right, as if they had ever followed that advice whenever there was something happening to me. Their kids always came first for them, so forget it, I was on my way to Pittsburgh on the next possible flight. I wanted to talk to the doctor myself, and go with Mom to her first chemotherapy session.

I told Mom I loved her, and she said she knew that, which choked me up even more. Here we all had thought that having to sell the house was this big, life-altering change. Little did we realize that that was merely a prelude to the real challenges that lay ahead.

CHAPTER THREE

Later that fateful morning, about an hour after I spoke to Mom, Keira called from Cleveland. She said she was going to take Mom to her first chemo session, and that she felt it would be best if I came into town a little later. After talking with Mom, Keira felt that though we all meant well, if we came swooping into Pittsburgh at the same time, it would only heighten the sense of stress for Mom. Keira argued that it would be best for us kids to stagger our visits, so that there was always one of us in town to help Mom and Dad out, but not so many that it felt like we were coming in for an emergency. Though it certainly did qualify as an emergency, and I hated the idea of having to stay in California while all this was going on, I realized that Keira was right. Mom had expressed to us that everyone must continue to live their own lives, and that we should all try to go about business as usual. I realized that the important thing here was Mom's comfort, not my own. I agreed to delay my trip back for a few days.

Melissa checked in after my call with Keira, and she was understandably upset. "Mom never smoked or drank, and what good did it do her? People might as well do whatever the hell they want!" she yelled in anguish. "Look, Mel," I said quietly, "The fact that Mom has taken such good care of herself is going to help her beat this. If she hadn't, she'd be in real trouble. And of course there's no guarantees in life, but it's smart to live as health-consciously as you can, to at least increase your odds."

I wasn't sure where this sound reasoning was coming from. Though I knew it was logical, I normally would have been more inclined to agree with Melissa's frightened, cynical thinking. I believed it was God, whom I don't even pretend to understand or comprehend, who was helping me calm my sister. At least, I hoped it was God, because I sensed we all were going to need a lot of His help in the months ahead.

Caitlin called next, and we talked about how shell-shocked we all were, yet how we were determined to do whatever we could to write a happy ending to this latest chapter in our lives. Caitlin agreed that we should avoid overwhelming Mom by all visiting at once, so we started making out a schedule for what days we'd each be able to "cover." Though Melissa lived in Pittsburgh, she had the least flexible schedule of any of us because of her job and her responsibilities with her sons. Luckily, the Residence would shuttle my mom back and forth to the place she'd get her chemo treatments, which coincidentally was right up the street from the Residence. It was ironic that we'd convinced them to accept assisted living in order to help Dad, and now Mom was the one who needed it most.

I went for a long walk in the park near my house, trying to clear my head and accept all that was happening. There happens to be a Senior Citizens Center on the park grounds, and I saw many elderly people being dropped off and picked up. Some were playing horseshoes, others sitting in wheelchairs at picnic benches leisurely enjoying the usual idyllic LA weather.

There were many elderly couples, and I thought of Dad and Mom and all their years together. I also noticed the many people who were by themselves, and couldn't help but think of Rita, and Heather, and me. Would I end up alone in my old age? Would either my dad or mom end up alone in their old age? I was flooded with an appreciation of how difficult life must become when one reaches the senior stages, not even counting the myriad of other difficulties that can come into play, such as Alzheimer's.

It seemed to be the very definition of irony that I was scheduled that night to perform a show about 'matchmaking' and here I was alone and in the process of perhaps losing a parent. I was completely filled with fear, anger, and hopelessness. I really wanted to cancel my show, just call in sick. But I knew that Mom would want me to go ahead with it. Besides, in my heart I believed Mom would overcome this, so I was determined to do exactly as she had asked, which was live my normal, abnormal life.

★★★★★★★★★★★

"Are you gonna move, or what?" Chester's good-natured voice shattered the silence at the LA Chess Club. "Yeah, back to Pittsburgh, as soon as my show wraps," I muttered. He could certainly empathize with my mom's situation, having lost his wife to cancer. He studied me a moment.

"Ed, like I told you before, there's no use in worrying. Her situation's in God's hands now."

"That's all you have to say to me?" I needled.

"Well, no. One more thing...checkmate." Hmm, apparently getting older not only makes a person wise, but it also makes them a wise-ass. We set up the pieces for another game.

"Seriously, Chester, I'm sort of freaking out here."

"No, you're not."

"Yes I am!" I insisted.

"Ed, you're here with me, playing chess, doing your shows, comforting your sisters, just living your life...that's not the sign of a guy freaking out. Standing up on a water tower with a sniper rifle, that's freaking out."

I laughed. "So as long as I'm not indiscriminately firing weapons in public places, I'm not freaking out?"

117

Chester nodded. "Now you got it." He pushed his queen's pawn ahead two spaces, then looked directly at me. "Ed, you're quite a bit younger than me, but you're still old enough to know by now that life is full of challenges. And the only way to keep those challenges from overwhelming you is to face them head on."

I nodded, then put my attention back onto the board. I moved my queen's pawn ahead two spaces, directly confronting Chester's pawn, and looked at him. "Just in case, though...do you know where the nearest water tower is?"

****

I walked with Mom into the oncologist's office. A week and a half into chemo, but she still looked pretty good. Though the treatments made her tired, she'd had very little of the nausea and other side effects that afflicted so many others in her situation. The doctors were extremely encouraged by what one of them characterized as "her remarkable progress in such a short time." Of course, all the nurses and other patients knew Mom by now. Though she was in the midst of immense challenges and faced plenty more ahead, she was her usual, incredibly positive and cheerful self around everyone, and you could just see those vibes spread. I pulled up a chair next to her as the nurse started the drip into her arm.

"So, what are they putting in you, Mom, is that whiskey?"

"I wish that's all it was, Eddie," she laughed.

Considering what was going on in this place, the atmosphere was remarkably upbeat. There were about ten other people getting their treatments, and it was a bright and airy room, with individual television sets for each patient. Some chatted with visitors, some slept, others read magazines. Wow, how could these people be so... casual, considering their situation? I mean, it was certainly better than sitting around screaming, for sure, but it was amazing to see cancer therapy being treated like another mundane errand for the day. And I couldn't help but notice the range of ages, from teenagers to people Mom's age.

I was moved by their plight, and the courage with which they faced it all. Looking at these patients was scary, touching, inspiring, humbling, all at the same time. Just like life itself.

Mom looked at me with a wry smile. "You know, when I first started coming here, I couldn't even look into the faces of the other people. I could barely utter the word 'cancer.' But I guess a person does what she has to do, and now I've gotten used to it. Strange, isn't it?"

"No, Mom, it's awesome. You rock!"

She smiled. "I assume that's good?"

"It's the best," I said, and squeezed her hand.

We sat quietly, until suddenly we heard, "Margaret? Ed?" We turned to see

Walter, another resident at the Broken Arms. A tall, lanky man with a ready smile and an extremely pleasant demeanor, he'd immediately become a favorite among our family, even though we didn't really know much about him. He never spoke about his background or family, and we never probed. It was surprising to run into him outside of the Residence.

"Well, hello Walter," Mom said cheerily. "What are you doing here?"

"Well, I'd like to say I'm just visiting somebody, but the truth is, I've just started chemotherapy."

"Really? Me, too. Welcome to the club."

Walter smiled. "There's sure a lot of us here, huh?" he said, surveying the room.

"Sure is," replied Mom. "And a fun time was had by all!"

Walter chuckled, and sat down for his treatment a couple stations over from us.

After Mom was finished with her treatment, the doctor told us he'd like to rest her from chemo for a few days, and reassess the situation from there. He said, "I assume you won't mind not having any toxic chemicals for awhile?" I said, "Hey, if she needs anything toxic, we'll let my sister Melissa cook for her!"

Mom wasn't about to argue with some time off. Though she was very brave, there was no doubt that the entire process was incredibly tough on her.

We headed back to the Residence, and Dad was happy to hear that she didn't have to go back for awhile. We were all cautiously optimistic with her progress at this point.

Dad had graduated from a cane to using a walker to get around now, the same walker he'd noticed someone else with when he and Mom first moved into the Residence. It was actually a really nice piece of equipment, and in fact Dad said the nurses told him, "It's considered the Cadillac of walkers." My sisters and I were really relieved he was using it, but we knew we shouldn't make a fuss about it, or Dad would stop using it out of stubbornness. It was funny watching us be nonchalant in front of him, but all of us exchanging thumbs up behind his back whenever he'd scoot acRonan the room in his "Cadillac."

Not surprisingly, Mom was feeling too weak to go to the dining area, but chef Deke was so nice that he asked us what she'd like to eat, and he brought it down to their apartment himself. He took pride in his work, as he should have, because it was great. I told him he should be proud of his work as a good human, too. He smiled. "I appreciate that, coming from you especially. Doing all that important stuff in Hollywood." I cringed. "Believe me, Deke, I've never done anything as important as the people around here do on a daily basis. I mean, what could possibly be more important than caring for others?"

"Well, you make people laugh, including your mom, and that's a nice way to care for others," Deke replied before excusing himself. I cut some of the food for Mom and sat with her as she slowly consumed what she could.

★★★★★★★★★★★★

"Well, folks, it's hard to believe, but I've been here for about six weeks now. Literally. I haven't left the building. They won't let me the hell out of here. For God's sake, somebody call the police." Laughter filled the Comedy Store, and it was gratifying to squint through the stage lights and see the outline of the sold-out crowd. It was my last show before a two-week hiatus from LA to take the show on the road. The great part was I'd be starting in Pittsburgh, with plans to go to Philly, New York, Columbus, Atlanta, then back to LA to finish my commitment at the Comedy Store.

"Dad and Mom are in assisted living. They can literally have someone feed them if they want. Apparently, I'm in unassisted living. I can't even get the clerk at McDonalds to wait on me."

I'm always bemused by the strange fact that the more frustrations I deal with in my personal life, the more fodder I have for my professional life in the form of material.

After an hour and a half, I was finished, and I disappeared backstage. Following the obligatory schmoozing with show-biz types, Ahmos and I went out for coffee, and discussed the upcoming tour. I was especially excited about Pittsburgh, and the timing of the run at the club where I had first started my career, the Funny Bone. I had two tickets to the Ohio State-Washington State game which was taking place in Columbus four days prior to the start of my shows in Pittsburgh. Thus, I planned to fly to Pittsburgh early, and drive my nephew Ronan to Ohio to take him to his first Buckeye game. As a bonus, Turk had procured tickets to the following Sunday's Steelers-Raiders game, which would be the perfect way to unwind after my shows Saturday night.

As I dragged myself into bed that evening, I was tired but happy. Dad had adjusted very well to the Friendship Residence, and hadn't fallen since he'd moved there. And Mom's condition seemed to improve all the time. Despite some swelling of her legs, her medical tests continued to give everyone reason for optimism. And soon, I'd be back home to see them both, and would get to partake of a virtual feast of football. Plus, I could finally start looking around for a house in Pittsburgh, on the sly, of course. I didn't want anyone to know I was coming back for good until everything was in place, but it soon would be. "Life should always feel this good," was my last conscious thought before drifting into a deep, peaceful sleep.

"You can't spell Chester without the word 'chess'," crowed the old man sitting across the board from me. He had me in deep shit, and we both knew it. I wasn't in the mood for his taunting. "Oh, really? You spell 'Chester' with two "s's", do you? Doesn't that just make you illiterate?" I grumbled.

"Wow, imagine your embarrassment. Getting creamed by an illiterate," he shot back.

Nuts. He'd surprised me with a move that led to a series of forcing variations, and it was clear that the momentum of his position was suddenly unstoppable. I smirked and tipped my King over, and allowed myself to relax.

"Great game, Chester. Man, I didn't see that Bishop move coming at all. I thought I'd looked really thoroughly at everything, but I didn't see it. "

Chester grinned. "Just because you didn't see it doesn't mean it wasn't there."

We set up for another game. "Okay, last one," I said. "I leave town tomorrow. I have to go home and pack."

"Wow, fleeing the city just to avoid playing me, huh?"

"Not to avoid playing you, to avoid *listening* to you."

Chester laughed, and pushed his queen bishop's pawn ahead two spaces. "So, how are your folks doing?," he asked.

"Pretty well, considering. There was a slight setback with Mom's condition, and the doctors put her back on chemo, but they're encouraged by her cell counts. They seem pretty sure they got it in time. And Mom's reacted very well to all the treatments so far, so hopefully that will remain the case."

I took a big swig of my coffee while I studied the board, then looked up to find Chester studying me intently.

"So, what else is on your mind, Ed?"

"My mom isn't enough?"

"It is, so why are you worrying about other things?"

Damn, no wonder he beat me so often. Apparently, he could read my mind.

"Well, I've been a little stressed over some of my work stuff, you know. There's so much I'd like to accomplish before my life is over."

"To distinguish yourself, I'm guessing?" Chester asked, as he made another move.

"Well, sure, yeah, I mean, everybody wants to leave some kind of legacy, right?" Chester thought a moment. "Well, true enough, but you know something? No matter what, at the end of the game, all the pieces go back in the same box."

As I made my next move, I noticed the time on my wristwatch and realized I had to get going. We agreed to a draw, shook hands, and made plans for a rematch as soon as I got back from my tour.

★★★★★★★★★★★

"This is awesome, Uncle Ed!" exclaimed Ronan, as we took our seats in

129

Ohio Stadium. He was absolutely right, it was awesome. A beautiful fall day, the renowned Ohio State marching band performing "Script Ohio," and a big game against Washington State about to take place. Ronan was as blown away by the surroundings as I had been when Dad had taken me to my first game at the "Horseshoe," and as undoubtedly Dad had been when his Dad had taken him to his first game, way back in the 1920's.

I had been taking Ronan's older brother Seamus, who was now fifteen, to games for the last several years, since the time he'd turned eleven. Now that Ronan was eleven, and had also become a big football fan, it was his turn to get into the rotation. Taking my nephew to a ballgame was just the sort of activity I would enjoy far more often once I moved back to Pittsburgh. After all, it was a rite of passage that my father had given to me, and that I was giving to my nephews, in lieu of children of my own. I still hoped to have kids someday, but I realized

I'd better take things one step at a time. Like, maybe meet a woman who would give me her real phone number.

I couldn't resist pulling out my cell phone and giving Dad a call. I knew he and Mom would be in front of their TV. Dad would be screaming at the game, and Mom would be trying to find me and Ronan, literally looking for two red needles in a 100,000-piece red haystack. Dad answered, but the reception was as bad as the one the crowd gave the Washington State team as they ran out onto the field.

"Dad, you're cutting in and out. Just wanted to let you know we're here."

"Yeah, I can barely hear you son, but we're watching. You guys have fun. You'll be back early tomorrow morning for brunch, right?"

"Absolutely! I----hello?" We got cut off, but it was just as well, as toe met leather and the ball flew high up into the crystal-clear blue sky. In my mind, I could hear legendary announcer Keith Jackson shouting, "We're underway!!"

Ronan and I knocked on Dad and
Mom's door at Friendship Residence the
next morning, and Ronan had his giant foam
finger ready to wave at them when they
opened the door. But nobody answered. We
knocked again, then heard Mom's voice,
telling us it was unlocked and to come on
in. I opened the door a crack, and Ronan
raced in and started high-fiving Dad and
Mom. "A big win for us, huh?" I said to Dad.
He nodded, and Mom smiled. But there was
something wrong. They were way too
subdued. I had a strange feeling. Before I
could say anything else, Mom turned to
Ronan. "Honey, can you go down and
reserve us a table for brunch? I need to talk
to your uncle." Ronan was happy to do so,
not picking up on the tension in the room.
He scampered off, leaving the three of us
sitting in the living room.
"What's going on, Mom?" I asked, my voice
filled with fear.

"I have some bad news, dear. The doctor called yesterday, and told me the cancer has spread too far, too fast. He told me I have only a few months to live, at most." I opened my mouth, but found myself unable to make a sound. I looked over at Dad, whose eyes seemed to be welling up, and he looked away, shaking his head. I looked back at Mom.

"Are you sure? No, that can't be. I want to talk to the doctor myself," I sputtered. But it was true. Mom's oncologist had sent some tests to the lab on Thursday, not expecting to find anything more serious than what already existed, but late Friday night, the tests came back with the ultimate nightmare scenario. The doctor had thus made a rare Saturday morning call to Mom with the news. And Mom, being the unbelievably unselfish and caring person that she was, didn't want to call and tell me and Ronan "because it would ruin our weekend in Columbus."

I was upset she hadn't told me sooner, but agreed that for Ronan' sake, maybe she was right.

"Does anyone else know? Keira, Coll, Melissa?"

"I told them all yesterday. Melissa wants to tell Ronan and Seamus herself." I fought back piping hot tears that formed instantly in the back of my eyes. "Mom, I don't know what to say, I'm...this can't be..." my voice trailed off and we all sat in silence. I walked over and hugged her. I didn't want to ever let her go, and yet, realized that sometime soon, I would have to do so forever.

A short while later, Melissa came over with Seamus, and we tried gamely to eat brunch and pretend nothing was wrong until Melissa could talk quietly with the kids in private. After our meal, Melissa drove back to her house with the boys to lay the news on them. I didn't envy her task. I sat with Dad and Mom in their apartment, trying, just as they were, to wrap my head around what was occurring. "I don't feel like I'm

134

dying," Mom suddenly blurted out. Indeed, she had been feeling much better in recent weeks, with the exception of her legs swelling, and had assumed, as we all did, that she was beating this thing. The doctors said that they couldn't believe she wasn't feeling worse, considering the amount of cancer in her poor body at this point. Mom was very calm, and almost philosophical. It was sad, moving, inspiring, surreal. "Well, I'm lucky and grateful to have lived to be eighty, but I have to admit, I feel greedy about it. I want to keep going, for at least another ten years or so. Just to spend some more time with you all."

I buried my face in my hands. Greedy? Mom had never had a greedy thought in her life. I was feeling greedy, though. I wanted my mom and dad around forever, and though I logically knew that was impossible, a part of me wanted to believe they would never die.

Mom told us what kind of funeral arrangements she wanted. She desired a "family only" funeral, and didn't want people visiting her at the funeral home, which I personally found a relief, as did Dad. He grew up with all the classic Irish wakes, where people party around the corpse as if it's a keg. (And kegs contain less booze than some of those corpses did.)

We all agreed that the best way to have family and friends pay their respects would be at a memorial mass at church. No casket on display, just a few pictures of Mom, the way people would always want to remember her.

"Mom, here's an idea," I said. "We should tell people you've already passed before you actually have."

"What are you talking about?"

"Well, then we can have the memorial mass, and during the ceremony, I'll stand up and say to the mourners, 'If only Mom could be here right now,' then you could suddenly walk out from behind the alter, and scare the hell out of everyone!"

Mom laughed while shaking her head, as if a bit ashamed of herself for laughing at such a thing. "Oh, Eddie, you're so silly, honestly!" She burst out laughing again, then Dad joined in, which made us all feel good, at least temporarily.

Ironically, Mom's gravesite was already set. My father, being the organized engineer that he is, had already paid for their indoor crypts, side by side, at a local Catholic mausoleum. He'd done so probably ten years earlier. He'd tried to get Mom to come look at the spots, but she wouldn't do it. She was glad he bought them, she just didn't want to actively participate in the situation. I couldn't blame her. Mom chuckled quietly, then turned to Dad. "Well, Ed, I guess I'm going to see the gravesite a lot sooner than I'd hoped. I still think it's cute that you bought 'above ground' plots because of my claustrophobia."
Mom and I laughed, and Dad looked at us sheepishly. "Well, what the hell, I think it makes sense."

"It's very considerate, Dad," I said, and Mom winked at me.

Dad said, "I wanted us to be in one place so that you kids can come visit us both at the same time."

"Oh, boy, Dad, how convenient. One-stop mourning. Maybe they can put in a drive-thru."

"Oh, Eddie, honestly, leave your poor father alone, won't you?" Mom pleaded with a laugh.

We sat quietly once again, and that's how it went, for the rest of the afternoon. We'd sit in silence for awhile, Mom would talk about what was in front of her, I'd make some ridiculous remark, we'd all laugh, then we'd sink back into silence. I think Dad and I felt more helpless than she did.

"Well, I'm canceling my shows here this week," I finally blurted out.

"No, you're not!" Mom shot back.

"But Mom, I can't—"

"Listen, Eddie, it's what you do, and you need to keep doing it. You need to live your life."

"But I need you to live your life, too, Mom," I coughed out.

"That's what I'm going to do. We don't know how long it will be, and I'm going to enjoy as normal a life as I possibly can."

"No, Mom, it doesn't seem right to be up there telling jokes when you're..."

"Please, honey, do your show."

I felt utterly confused. Mom took a long pause, then added, "For me."

I turned to her. "Okay, fine," I said, resignedly. "Man, I can't believe you guys have turned into pushy show-biz parents! The next thing you know, Dad's gonna start teeing off on me with his belt, like Michael Jackson's father did to him."

"If I thought it would make you write funnier jokes, I'd do it," Dad laughed.

We sat listening to the birds outside, and the steady ticking of their grandfather clock. Ugh. I could literally hear the seconds

139

of Mom's life, and all our lives for that matter, ticking away. Finally, I offered, "Mom, you don't know how long you could live. It could be years, you hear those stories all the time. You know, a doctor gives some guy a day to live, then years later, that guy ends up giving the eulogy at the doctor's funeral."

"Oh, Eddie," Mom chuckled. "I don't think that will happen. Dr. Montini is a healthy young man! Besides, I wouldn't want to give anyone's eulogy!"

"Hey, better to give one than get one, right?" I joked. Mom smiled wanly.

The next morning, I did call Mom's doctor, just to double check and triple check and hip check and whatever kind of check I could do to maybe get a reversal of the death sentence that had been so unjustly handed out to my mother. Unfortunately, the doctor merely confirmed Mom's words, and he told me it could really be anytime from a few weeks to six or eight months. I asked for his best guess, and he sighed. "Honestly? Sooner rather than later. I recommend setting things up with the hospice people."

****

Mom and I strolled up and down the hallway outside their apartment. She told me she wanted to get some exercise, adding wistfully, "Although, I'm not sure what for!" We went back and forth, up and down the same stretch of hallway. Nobody else was around, everyone in their rooms, or down in the cafeteria. Mom walked slower than she used to because of the swelling the cancer had caused in her legs. She told me it was getting harder to sit comfortably in her favorite chair, which we'd brought over in the move from the Tyris house. I told her that I could go get her a new chair, one that was stiffer, with a footrest, one that would be easier for her to get in and out of. She liked the idea, and so did I. For the first time that day, I felt like I could actually do something, anything, to help her. We paced back and forth in silence some more, and suddenly Mom stopped and looked me in the eye.

"I'm sorry we didn't do more for you, Eddie."

"What are you talking about, Mom? What more could you possibly have done? Well, outside of actually giving me that Porsche I asked for when I got my driver's license."

Mom smiled at the memory of that earnest but preposterous request I had made as a sixteen-year-old. She said, "Well, I don't know, dear. Maybe we could have put you into some sort of school for the arts or something."

"Mom, I would have had no interest in such a thing. I'm not an artist. I'm just a comedian."

She smiled again. "You've been a comedian since the day you were born. You're our gift of laughter from God."

As tears formed in my eyes, I was taken aback, albeit in a good way, by this remark. In my mind, I'd caused my parents far too much worry over the years, between the sheer uncertainty of my chosen career, and my ferocious bout with alcoholism. But I was grateful they were able to see me get sober, and watch my career take off. Fortunately, overall things had worked out pretty well for me, at least in Mom's lifetime, both personally and professionally. "Mom, I'm not just saying this, but regarding how you've raised me, I seriously wouldn't change one thing. Whatever success I've had is directly because of you and Dad. I really couldn't imagine having better parents. I'm so thankful to you both."

Tears began rolling down Mom's face, and she turned to me and said, "Dear, you were always good about telling us that. You always told us how much you loved us, and we are grateful for that."

Now it was my turn for tears to roll.

"You know, dear," she continued. "I'm sorry you haven't met someone to settle down with. I know it hurts you."

The remark came as quite a surprise. Here I thought I'd always hidden most of my pain over my broken engagement from Mom, to spare her more worry. Proof once again that no child possesses the stealth necessary to fly under a mother's radar.

"Mom, I haven't given up or anything," I said softly.

"Oh, I know, and you shouldn't. But I'm just sorry it's turned out to be more difficult than you would have liked."

"Well, lots of things turn out more difficult than any of us would like, Mom. I have no regrets."

Actually, that was a lie. I did have some *enormous* regrets. I knew it was illogical, but I couldn't help myself from suddenly feeling immense anger at my ex-fiancée, feeling that if she hadn't spent all those Christmas' with me and my folks, my *real* wife-to-be could have been there. Now, whoever that was going to be, if indeed I ever did find her, would never meet my mother. And, my kids, if indeed I ever did have them, would never know their grandmother. These thoughts were almost too much to bear. Yep, I had plenty of regrets, but I didn't want Mom to know about it.

"I wish that was true, Eddie, but I know you have regrets. It's okay. But the relationships that didn't work out, that were painful to you, are actually a blessing, because those relationships weren't meant to be."

"I guess not, Mom.""

"Don't be discouraged, what's meant to happen, will happen."

"Yeah, but what if what's meant to happen is something terrible? Like...." My suddenly shaky voice trailed off.

"Like my getting cancer?"

I nodded solemnly, and Mom sighed, then continued. "Well, I have to admit I don't see much good about it, but just because I

145

don't see it doesn't mean it isn't so. All we can do is accept what's handed to us."

I gave her a hug, and we continued to walk the hallways in silence for a long time.

★★★★★★★★★★★★

Caitlin came in from New York, ostensibly to see my shows at the Funny Bone, but in reality, wanting to spend some time with our mother. We decided we'd go to a furniture store and get that new chair for Mom. Dad insisted we use his credit card to make the purchase. I laughed to myself, knowing that no matter the price, Dad would be surprised. Dad is as smart as they come, but because Mom has always done all the shopping over the years, he's remarkably unaware of the price of just about everything. It's not that he's cheap, but he'd sort of lost track of the rate of inflation since 1950. He'd send me out to pick up a new telephone, and ask, "What do you need, ten bucks or so?" I'd reply, "Dad, for ten bucks, I can probably get you two cups and a string." He handed Caitlin and I his credit card, and, right on cue, asked, "So what's a new chair, a hundred bucks or so?" Caitlin stifled a giggle and told him we'd do the best we could.

Caitlin and I found what we believed to be the holy grail of chairdom, and loaded it into her car. I smiled again thinking about Dad, as the Visa card was swiped for the $600 charge. Just as we were about to drive away, the clerk who'd waited on us came running out and stopped us.
"Hey, I'm sorry," he said breathlessly. "I overcharged you five dollars because I accidentally entered the wrong code in the register. If you don't mind coming back in, I'll run your card again, and I'll actually give you ten dollars off for the inconvenience."
It certainly was difficult to picture this exchange taking place back in LA. Acts of honesty and kindness seemed to be frequent and appreciated in Pittsburgh,

unlike Hollywood, where honesty is often viewed with suspicion, if not outright hostility.

As an example, one afternoon I'd gone to the grocery store in my LA neighborhood, and as I was loading everything into the trunk of my car, I realized there was a stick of deodorant that I hadn't taken out of the shopping cart, and thus hadn't been charged for. It cost less than two bucks, but right is right, and RightGuard is RightGuard, so I knew I needed to go back and pay for it. One of the worst things about having a conscience is the sheer inconvenience of it all.

I sighed disgustedly, and trudged back inside the store. I was going to go back to the clerk who had just waited on me, but saw that at his station there was suddenly a line so long that I can only assume they were handing out free diamonds. So I got in the express lane, even though there were quite a few people in that line as well.

148

Not surprisingly, the "express" lane was moving about as fast as the "express" lane on the freeway does, that's to say, not at all. I looked at my watch, and briefly entertained the thought of just heaving the deodorant across the store and leaving. That wouldn't be stealing, after all. But, I needed the product, and I was already there, so what the hell. I realized I might have to pick up some razors, too. I had plenty at home, but figured I'd need to shave again by the time I got through this line.

After what seemed like an eternity, I finally reached the clerk, and started to sputter out the story that I'd been in here before and forgot to pay for this, but caught myself. Why would she care? Hey, *I* didn't even care. So I just plopped the RightGuard up on the conveyor, and she rang it up. Of course, I had to read the register to find out what I owed, as some clerks these days seem to have a real aversion to actually verbalizing the cost of the purchase.

I attempted to make eye contact with her on the off chance that she might actually want to speak to me, but she looked away disinterestedly. Too bad she didn't work her job with the same enthusiasm as she was working her chewing gum.

I saw that the machine read "$1.62," so I dug into my wallet and handed her two singles.

"Out of two," she announced somberly. Then, with a smirk, she asked, "Was this an emergency purchase?"

"What do you mean?"

"Well, you came to the store just to buy a stick of deodorant? Did you need it right away?"

I resisted the temptation to peel my shirt off, jam it in her face and yell, "I don't know, you tell me!!" Instead, I just shook my head "no" and smiled.

She stuffed my two dollars into the register and handed me the deodorant. "Do you need a bag?" she asked with a laugh.

"Yes, and a gift box, too."

"Really?" she asked, giving me a confused look.

"No, I'm kidding."

"Next," she called out.

I took the deodorant and was about to leave when I realized that I hadn't received my change.

"Excuse me, I didn't get any change."

"It comes out of that thing," she said, pointing to one of those chute and cup doohickeys that spits the coins at the customers. Another life-saving invention that shields folks from having to engage in any of that unpleasant human interaction.

"Well, nothing came out of there," I continued.

She eyed me suspiciously. "It should have," she answered.

"I don't doubt that, but it didn't."

I should have just left the store, but the indignities were piling up too high at this point. Suddenly, these thirty-eight cents felt like the most important sum of money I'd ever been involved with.

She told me to wait, then went to get her manager. This made me even more popular with the people waiting in line behind me. I kept my back to them, but I could hear their muttering. The manager approached me.

"My employee says she pressed the change button, but she says you say you didn't get it."

"I don't get *any* of this," I answered. "Do you really think I'm trying to cheat you guys out of thirty-eight cents?"

By now, most of the people in the store were staring at me. I've worked on television shows that didn't have this many people watching. Then, the clerk who had waited on me earlier recognized me.

"Hey," he said. "I scanned that guy out just a few minutes ago. Why is he back in here?"

"Because I forgot to pay for this," I stammered, waving the deodorant stick aloft, just in case I didn't look foolish enough already. "I'm just trying to pay for this."

The manager looked at me with contempt. "What kind of person comes all the way back to pay for one little thing?"

"Apparently, a stupid one," I answered. Eventually, I left with my proper change, head held high. It felt good to finally know the price of my own dignity: thirty-eight cents.

The freshly discounted chair turned out to be a smash hit when Caitlin and I got it back to the Friendship Residence. I could only hope I'd be as big a hit when I did my shows that night. I was not really in the frame of mind to perform, but honoring Mom's request, I did my best. As I recall, the shows went well, though they felt a bit dreamlike, and I had practically no recollection afterwards. It was like being abducted by a space craft, thankfully minus the anal probe that is apparently mandatory during interactions with alien space travelers.

I was relieved the shows were over, and was grateful that I had only booked one night. I don't think I could have done any more shows, no matter what Mom would've asked of me. And at that point, without telling her, I postponed the rest of my tour indefinitely.

I secretly arranged to meet with a realtor in Pittsburgh. I would have used Helen, the woman who sold my folks' place, but I was paranoid that she might accidentally tell someone who knew me that I was in the market. So I randomly stopped into a local real estate office, and got hooked up with an eager new rep named Danny. I described to him the kind of property and amenities I was looking for, and I must have been a pretty undemanding customer, because in response to everything I requested, he nodded his head furiously and said, "Right, right, right, right..." in rapid fire manner, like a frightened passenger trying to give a confused driver directions. He told me he had "the perfect house" for me, and we got in his car and headed off to see it in person.

As we pulled up to the property, Danny turned to me.

"You'll love this, it's just like out West!" he chortled gleefully.

"Well, that's interesting," I replied.

"According to you realtors, the houses out West are 'just like back East,' and the houses out East are 'just like out West.' No wonder American kids score so low on geography exams."

Danny chuckled, but didn't disagree, and as we got out of his car, I scanned the area.

"So Danny, where's the driveway?" I asked.

"Aw, you don't need it. There's plenty of space on the street," he replied, with a dismissive wave of his hand.

"But wasn't that the first thing I mentioned as being a necessity?"

"Right, right, right, right...don't worry, there's room to build one, but you don't need it."

Well, maybe he was right. Or should I say, "right, right, right, right." After all, this house was on a cul-de-sac, and there did appear to be plenty of space on the street. I just hoped Henrietta didn't have any relatives living in the neighborhood.

Danny keyed us in through the front door, and we were greeted with the sight of lots of sawdust and carpenter's tools still lying around. Which would have been understandable if the house was brand new, but it had been built twenty years ago.

"What's all this?" I asked, pointing to a wall over the staircase that was partially torn out.

"Oh, the owner likes to tinker with the house himself."

"Well, Danny, to me, 'tinkering' is maybe putting a new faucet in the bathroom. Not knocking down walls."

"Don't worry, the guy knows what he's doing."

"Is he a contractor?"

"No, an accountant."

"What, did he stay at a Holiday Inn last night?" I asked incredulously.

Danny smirked, then his sprinkler-like cadence went off again. "Right, right, right, right, don't worry, he'll fix the wall, but you don't need it."

"I don't need a wall?"

"Not really, not there. It's cool to actually be able to see the staircase, you know? Like "Gone with the Wind."

Which is what I'm soon going to be, I thought. "Let's look at the back yard," I said.

Danny's skull started nodding like a bobblehead doll in an earthquake. "Right,

right, right, right!" We walked to the back door, and he opened the blinds to reveal…a giant cement and brick patio. There was not an inch of greenery to be seen anywhere. This must be what Al Gore's nightmares look like.

"Where's the grass?"

"You don't need it. All that upkeep…it's better to have brick."

It's a good thing Danny knew what I needed, because clearly I didn't.

He took me back inside the house.

"It's a little stuffy in here," I commented. "Can we flip on the AC?"

"Oh, it doesn't have central air."

"Danny, I have to have central air, for crying out loud…"

"You don't need it. You just open windows here. It doesn't get that hot, it's not like California."

"But didn't you say it was 'just like out West'?"

"Let's check out the kitchen," Danny said quickly.

158

"It has a kitchen? Wow, I have to say I'm surprised at this point," I muttered. Had he listened to *anything* I'd asked for when we were back in his office? The rattling sound from his furiously nodding head must have drowned out everything I'd said to him. "That's okay, Danny, I think I've seen enough."

Danny continued to be the very definition of oblivion.

"So, should we put in an offer on this baby?" he asked cheerfully.

"Um, no...we should put in a driveway, then a yard, then central air, then a new wall. Then, maybe an offer."

Danny nodded. "Okay, that's cool. I've got some other perfect properties, too."

Other perfect ones? Well, I guess this one *was* pretty much perfect. I mean, other than not having any of the qualities I was looking for, it was perfect for me.

"Well, thanks Danny, I'm out of time today, but I'll call you next time I'm in town, okay?" I sounded like Charlie Sheen blowing off some one-night stand. But Danny didn't seem bothered, and gave me one more "right, right, right, right," for the road.

I stayed for a few more days in Pittsburgh than I'd originally planned, but Mom finally insisted that I go back to LA and maintain my usual schedule. I didn't argue too much, because my realtor in LA had called and told me there were several serious inquiries into my house, and he needed me out there. Fortunately for me, it was a seller's market in California, and it looked like I could make a decent profit on my house. That is, as long as nobody found out about their potential neighbor Henrietta. If she happened to confront some prospective buyer for parking in "her" space, I'd have a better chance of selling my place if it was located on top of an old Indian burial ground.

I told Mom that from now on, I would be coming back to Pittsburgh about every ten days or so. She naturally protested, saying that I had to keep up with my responsibilities in LA. But I assured her I'd be able to do my work and still get back to Pittsburgh quite often. None of us knew how much time she had left in this world, and I was determined to spend every minute I could with her. Even in my sometimes-self-absorbed little Hollywood world, it was clear that helping care for Mom was a slightly bigger responsibility than coming up with a funny quip for the wacky neighbor on some sit-com.

CHAPTER FOUR

I reached into the bookshelf in my den and pulled out a copy of "Just The Facts!" Though it sounds like a Jack Webb biography, it in fact is a book on chess endgames, written by Grandmaster Lev Alburt. I flipped it open, and saw the inscription on the title page, signed by the author. "*To Margaret, many great endgames! Lev Alburt.*" I laughed at the memory. Mom had ordered the book for my thirty-ninth birthday, and had sent a note asking for Grandmaster Alburt to autograph it. But she'd forgotten to mention it was for her son, and Alburt naturally looked at the name on the check, and inscribed the book to "Margaret." Mom had been really embarrassed when she'd realized what had happened, but there wasn't time to replace the book before my birthday, so she gave it to me as was. Of course, I was happier that it said "Margaret" than I would have been had it read "Eddie," because it was something else for me to tease her about. "I knew you'd enjoy that, Eddie," she'd chuckled ruefully.

Reading through the book inspired me to drive over to the LA Chess Club. Though I'd been back in Los Angeles for almost a week, I had been too busy catching up on my work to make it over to the club. I'd gotten a movie "punch-up" gig, which entailed writing jokes and funny scenes for a script that was already in production. The latest project was an animated movie, which was fun, and interestingly, much of the acting was actually *less* cartoonish than that of some human actors I'd worked with. Because of deadlines that are necessary for companies to put animation together, and the fact that I'd taken extra time back in Pittsburgh to be with my family, I was way behind where I was supposed to be. I basically ended up cramming two weeks' work into one week. I was mentally and physically exhausted, but happy for the distraction, and pleased that the producers

163

seemed to like my contributions. But I was definitely ready to recharge my batteries by getting engrossed in some spirited games of chess.

As I entered the club, I nodded to several of the regulars, who acknowledged me briefly before aiming their concentration back at their boards. I looked around for Chester, but didn't see him. I glanced at my watch. Hmm, he was usually here around this time. I wandered around the club and watched some of the other games in progress. I spotted the president, Michael, working on some tournament charts in the corner.

"Hey, Michael, what's up?"

"Hi, Ed. Where ya been?"

"Oh, uh, busy out of town, busy in town. Just... busy, I guess."

"Well, that's a good thing, isn't it?"

"Absolutely, especially in this economy. Hey, have you seen Chester?"

Michael looked at me quizzically. "Chester?" he asked.

I laughed and said, "Yeah, you know, old guy, cheats like hell, but still can't beat me?"

Michael just stared at me, and I suddenly got a sick feeling in my stomach.

"Ed, I'm sorry, I thought you knew. Chester passed away."

I felt like someone had just slapped me in the face. "What are you talking about?" I sputtered.

Michael went on to explain that Chester had had a sudden heart attack at his house one night, if one can describe a heart attack in one's mid-eighties as "sudden." I felt the color drain from my face. I asked about services, but everything had already happened, while I was away. Chester was literally dead and buried. I slumped into a chair opposite Michael. Shit, I thought, what was with all this death stuff? Honest to God, what am I, the grim reaper?

I asked Michael if there was a place where I could send flowers, or a donation, or something. It was only then that I realized, I didn't even know Chester's last name.

I wandered aimlessly through the rows of people playing chess, somehow thinking that I might find Chester at one of the boards, and he'd laugh and say, "Gotcha! Thought I was dead, huh? Well, you're gonna wish I was when I show you my new opening move. Sit down and prepare for the thrashing of your life!" I smiled in spite of myself because I could truly hear his voice in my head. But to know that I'd never again hear his voice in my ears was almost impossible to comprehend.

I took a deep breath and tried to analyze my new position. What would Chester tell me to do? He'd probably say, stop regretting what the position isn't, and start pushing forward to make the best of how the board actually stands now. And I'd say, sure, but that's easier said than done. He'd say, if all else fails, just talk about your feelings. And I normally would...to Chester.

But now I couldn't anymore. The world was suddenly a much scarier, confusing place.

Back at my house that afternoon, I called Mom, as I had done every day since I'd last seen her. She was trying her best to sound upbeat, but I could hear the strain in her voice, a strain once again not caused by any particular physical discomfort, but a product of knowing her passing was inexorably approaching. She raved about the hospice people, particularly her nurse, Sharon. I had called Sharon when she first started treating Mom, just to introduce myself, and asked if there was anything I could do. Sharon was an incredible person, as one would almost have to be in her line of work. She stopped in to see Mom every other day or so, to check her vital signs, and see if Mom needed anything. Sometimes she'd give Mom medication to help reduce the swelling in her legs, but the most therapeutic part of their visits was the chats they'd have. Sharon told me that

167

Mom always made her feel so cheerful by the time she was finished visiting that the matter of just who was getting the most therapeutic help out of the visits was debatable.

"Well, I'll let you go, Mom. I've got to take care of some stuff out here, but I'll be seeing you in just a few days."

"I'm looking forward to it, Eddie."

✶✶✶✶✶✶✶✶✶✶✶

As I stood outside the Pittsburgh airport with my luggage, I buttoned my jacket up against the late October chill. I knew that I had been spoiled by living in sunny California for the last few years, but this seemed unusually cold, even for this time of year. Turk honked as he pulled into the passenger pick-up area, and I jumped into his car.

"Well, happy forty-first, old man."

"I'm not forty-one yet, pal," I snapped. "I've still got a day."

"Oh, right, you do. My bad. So, you want to do one last fun thing while you're still young?"

"If it involves me putting a gag on you, I'm all for it."

"You'd do that for me? Wow, I have to pay good money to have that done to me downtown."

"I didn't say I'd do it for free."

We guffawed liked college sophomores, and inside, I sort of wished I *was* back in college. Things seemed easier then, at least, in some ways. I know for sure I wasn't worrying about my parents' mortality back then. Nor my own, for that matter.

Turk dropped me at the Broken Arms, and Mom and Dad were waiting for me, sitting in their chairs. Dad and I shook hands, and Mom stood up to hug me. I was surprised by the obvious exertion it took her to get to her feet. It was clear the cancer was beginning to rob her of much of her physical strength. Her spirits seemed good, however, as we sat and talked. They

169

asked how the flight was, and we joked about my luggage. I'd had more than my share of lost and delayed luggage over the years, and it was always a topic for humorous discussion whenever I visited. I almost felt bad that I didn't have a baggage screw-up to report, but everything had been surprisingly smooth this time in. "Don't worry," I reassured them, "I'm sure they'll mess it up when I go back to LA. Some confused villagers in Thailand will be picking through my clothes as I stand in line at an airline counter to fill out a bunch of forms."

I was struck with a sense of déjà vu, a really nice kind. This scene had played out countless times over the years, me coming back to see the folks, them both sitting in their chairs, me plopped on the couch. We'd start with jokes about my airplane trip, then catch up on the lives of our relatives and friends. The only thing different was that instead of taking place at the Tyris house, it was at the Friendship Residence. That, and the fact that my mom was dying.

Oh, yeah, that. No matter how hard we all tried, cancer's specter dominated the room like the drunken, clueless party guest who doesn't realize everyone else has gone home. Finally, I found the courage to bring up something I'd been thinking about quite a bit over the preceding few days. "Mom," I started, then stopped, then started again. "I have something sort of odd to ask of you, but I need to do it, I think." Mom looked at me with a quizzical expression. "What is it, Eddie?"

"Well, when you...when you, uh..."

"Die?" Mom said firmly.

"Um, when you pass away, if you can, just to let me know everything is okay, can you give me a sign?"

"Well, goodness, dear, I don't know if I can. What kind of sign?"

"Well, it's okay if you can't, if they don't let you, or whatever. But, if you have a chance,

171

can you move a chess piece on the board in my living room?"

She and Dad both laughed, and suddenly I felt sheepish. I'd recently seen a special on A&E about people who'd had supernatural experiences, and one of the stories dealt with a man who'd visited his father on his deathbed, and asked him to give him a sign that he was okay when he passed over. Several days after his dad's death, the man had walked into his bedroom to discover that somehow his dad's American flag had been folded up, and was resting in a completely different place than it had been earlier that day.

"Oh, Eddie, I don't know if I'll actually be able to do that. I think you'll feel I'm around, but it will probably be more of something you sense, instead of something physical like that."

"I understand, Mom, and I won't be mad if you can't. But if you can, just a pawn or something, I just wanted to bring it up before, you know, just so..."

My voice trailed off, and Mom smiled at me. "Certainly dear, if I can, I will."

Dad wore an expression of bemusement, then sort of looked at me as if I was a little boy who just didn't understand all that was happening.

It was getting late, and I knew my folks wanted to go to bed, so I said my good-nights.

"We'll see you tomorrow for your birthday brunch, Eddie."

"Thanks, Mom, I'm looking forward to it. Not so much the getting older part, but the brunch part, anyway."

I took their car and drove up the street to Turk's. I really was looking forward to the next day, mostly because not only was I coming to brunch at the Friendship Residence, but Mom and Dad had invited Turk, Ann, and their kids too, as well as Melissa and her boys. Chef Deke always had great food, especially on Sundays, and being with my friends and family was the only birthday present I really wanted.

When I knocked on my folks' door about ten the next morning, Keira, who'd driven in from Cleveland for the day, answered. She didn't look too good.

"Hi, Keira, what's going on?"

"Um, Mom had a rough night. I guess she suddenly woke up feeling really dizzy and nauseous. The hospice people came over, and she's just gotten to sleep now."

I walked into the apartment, where Melissa was standing, looking grim.   A subdued Seamus and Ronan sat quietly on the couch. Dad looked up at me from his chair.

"Happy Birthday, Big Ed."

"Thanks, Dad. So, what's going on?"

Melissa filled me in on the rest of the details. Sharon had assured her that Mom was okay for now, that this was just an inevitable symptom of her condition. Mom needed rest. I walked back and peeked into the bedroom, and saw Mom sleeping soundly. I pulled the door closed, and went back into the family room.

"Should I tell Turk and Ann not to come?" I asked Dad.

"No, no, we want to have brunch. It's your birthday, Big Ed. We'll all go. We can bring your mom back something to eat later. Let's let her sleep."

There was that old adage again: "The show must go on."

I looked at my nephews. They were so mellow it was spooking me. Usually they'd be wrestling each other, and laying down the gauntlet of who was going to eat the most. I couldn't take this serenity a minute longer. I started wrestling with them, and they started to giggle and perk up. Dad and Melissa seemed relieved that the silence was broken. In mock anger, Dad said, "Okay, you kids, and I don't know who's the kids and who's supposed to be the adult there. But let's take it down the hall, we don't want to wake Grandma."

Turk and his family arrived as we entered the dining hall. We told them Mom was under the weather. They were sad to hear that, as were the workers and other residents of the facility. The Friendship Residence really was like a small town, and when someone wasn't there that was supposed to be, everyone noticed and inquired about it. It was nice in a certain way, because it was sincere, but in another way, it was very unpleasant, because I didn't want to have to tell even one more person that Mom wasn't feeling well. It was bad enough that the thought was racing through my brain on an endless loop. I didn't want to have to verbalize it over and over again, too.

In spite of the circumstances, we all had a nice meal together. Turk's daughters and three-year-old son Darren really perked everyone up. The residents always enjoyed seeing children running around. Dad got a particular kick out of how much food Darren was able to eat. "He puts away more than I do!" Dad observed with delight. Turk, who also could eat with the best of them, beamed, "That's my boy!"

Ann said, "He's always been a good eater. He was no fun to clean up after. Thank God he's out of diapers!"

"I wish I could say the same!" shot back Dad. We all cracked up, including Deke, who'd stopped by the table to say hello and was privy to the whole conversation. "Can I fix something for you to take back to Margaret?" he asked Dad.

"No thanks, Deke. She just needs to rest now."

"Okay, but if you need anything, or she wakes up hungry, or whatever, just give me a holler."

Several hours later, I sat with Dad and Keira, watching football on TV with the volume down very low. Melissa and the kids had gone back home, as had Turk and his family. Mom was still resting, and Dad and I were doing our best not to scream at the game like we normally would. During halftime, I wandered back to the bedroom to check on Mom, and as I poked my head in the door, she opened her eyes.

"Oh, Eddie, hi," she said groggily. "What time is it?"

"It's a little after three in the afternoon, Mom. How do you feel?"

"Oh, okay, just tired. Oh no, did I miss the brunch?"

"Well, yeah, Mom, but we didn't want to wake you. Sharon told us you needed to rest, so we let you sleep. Although I had to talk Seamus and Ronan out of coming in here and putting your hand in a bowl of warm water."

She smiled, then suddenly frowned. "Oh, no, did Turk's family come over? Oh, it's rude of me to not be there."

"Yep, they did, Mom, and they spent the entire time talking about how rude it was of you to not feel well," I chided. "Seriously, they were really sorry they didn't get to see you, but sent their best regards." I asked her if she was hungry, and she said she was. I walked down to the kitchen and

178

asked Deke for a couple poached eggs, which he was more than happy to whip up for her.

Mom sat up in bed and ate, and seemed to be regaining some of her color. She insisted that Dad and I go back to watching the football game, so Keira went into the bedroom and sat with Mom for awhile. A little later, Keira came back out into the family room, and told us Mom was sleeping again. We figured that was a good thing. Keira was due to drive back to Cleveland because she had to work the next morning, but was hesitant about leaving, considering the sort of day Mom had had.

We talked about it, and finally agreed that since Mom seemed much better, it would probably be best for Keira to go back home as planned. I'd keep an eye on Mom for the rest of the day, and if anything weird occurred, I'd let Keira know. We called Sharon from the hospice, and she told us she thought Mom was okay for now, and that she'd come by the next morning to check on her. Dad insisted Keira take off, because he didn't want her driving when it was dark. I was certain he was aware that Keira's car had headlights, but he had this thing about night-driving, so Keira humored him and hit the road.

Dad and I sat and watched the World Series that night, a tense game between the Angels and Giants, as Mom continued to sleep in the bedroom. I figured I'd see Dad off to bed after the game, and make my way back to Turk's, once I was sure he and Mom were okay for the night. And I was definitely eager to chat with Sharon the next morning, to get her professional take on all that had occurred that day. Suddenly, we heard Mom stir, and with great effort, Dad pushed himself to his feet and wheeled his walker back to see her. I walked back, too, and Mom sat up and looked at us.

"Goodness, what time is it?"

"It's about nine, honey," said Dad.

"I shouldn't be sleeping all day," she continued.

"Hey, you're lazy Mom, we all know that." She smiled at me. "Happy Birthday, Eddie! Oh, no, did I miss brunch?"

Dad and I exchanged looks.

"Yeah, Mom, but that's okay."

She looked a bit confused. "Did Turk and his family come over?"

This was now officially unnerving. "Yes, Mom, don't you remember me telling you that before?"

"No, dear. You did?"

"It's okay, Mom. I forget things every day, too. How do you feel?"

She told us she felt weak and tired, and we encouraged her to go back to sleep. She did, and Dad and I went back into the family room. I expressed my concern over Mom's confusion, though Dad shrugged it off. But I determined that I was going to stay overnight on their couch. I knew the

Friendship Residence had its own medical personnel twenty-four hours a day, but I didn't feel comfortable going back to Turk's with Mom still appearing to be a bit foggy. I looked over at my father, braced myself, then spoke:

"Dad, I think I should stick around tonight."

"Well, okay."

There were several beats of silence, and I realized to my surprise that Dad wasn't going to try to talk me out of staying. Instead, he sank back in his chair, closed his eyes, and sighed.

"I'm so tired."

"Well, why don't you go get some sleep, Dad?"

"Nah, I want to watch the rest of the baseball game." He looked at me, and I nodded. He drew his eyes back to the TV, but it was obvious he was having a hard time keeping them open, even for the World Series.

Within a few minutes, he had fallen asleep.

I watched a pitch, then looked over at my sleeping father, then watched another pitch, and again over to my father. Finally, I walked over to him and nudged him awake. "Dad...you should go to bed. I'll tell you what, I'll pop in a tape and record the rest of the game. You can watch it in the morning."

He groggily agreed, and made his way into the bedroom where he put himself in the twin bed next to Mom's.

I sat and watched the game, but was distracted with concern for what was going on. Was Mom suddenly in trouble, or was this just a hiccup along the way? Was this the start of her really beginning to get sick, or was she just having a tough day? I tried not to obsess too much on it. Shit, what a birthday.

I watched the Angels pull out a dramatic win, then watched some of the post-game analysis. I finally turned off the television shortly after midnight, and tried to get comfortable on the couch so I could get some sleep. Just as I was nodding off, I heard someone stir. I ran into the bedroom to see Mom sitting up in bed with one foot on the floor, looking pretty shaky.

"Mom, what's going on? Are you okay?" I whispered.

"Yes, dear, I'm going to the bathroom."

I dashed over to help her. She was really weak, and I lifted her up and draped her arm around my neck. I told her I'd take her into the bathroom.

She said softly, "Okay, we're going to the church over there, right?"

I looked at her. "What are you talking about, Mom?"

"We're going to the church over there, right? I see it."

My stomach knotted instantly. Clearly she was completely confused.

"Come on, Mom, I'm taking you to the bathroom."

She started leading me the wrong way, away from the door leading to the toilet.

"No, Mom, this way. Come on, I'm right here."

I gently turned her in the proper direction. "Are Turk and Ann coming over for brunch today?" she asked.

I felt the cold grip of utter fear envelope my entire body. Oh my God. This was serious. Mom was in huge trouble. She was completely incoherent. I knew this was the beginning of the end.

As we made our way slowly out of the bedroom, suddenly Dad lurched awake. He was clearly still mostly asleep, and without his glasses, he squinted at us for a moment. "Hey, Big Ed. Who won the game?"

God bless Dad. The poor guy had no idea what was happening at this instant with Mom, and asked the first natural question that came to mind.

"Um, the Angels. Tim Salmon hit a two-run homer in the eighth, and they won 11-10."

"Wow, how about that," Dad mumbled, then immediately fell back to sleep. In the midst of the sheer terror that gripped me over what was happening to Mom, I was grateful for this moment of Dad just being Dad. It was oddly comforting, his asking about the ballgame without another care in the world, not aware in the slightest of the serious events that were engulfing Mom.

I helped Mom onto the toilet, then stepped out into the hall to give her some privacy. She was able to urinate, but then became too disoriented to stand back up. I helped her to her feet, and began walking her back to the bedroom. She began speaking more gibberish, at least, it was gibberish to me. A hodgepodge of statements about brunch, and church, and Turk and his family. I helped Mom into the bedroom, where Dad was snoring away at top volume. Mom looked at me and asked, "Wow, listen to that snoring! Is that your dad, or Breezy?"

186

I suddenly remembered how our dog Breezy used to snore, too, and how we'd often joke about who was louder, she or Dad. "I think it's Dad, Mom," I said quietly. I helped her into bed, and she fell asleep almost immediately. I sat up on the couch for the rest of the night, trying to understand what was happening, and trying to figure out what I should, or could, do about it all.

Dad woke up early that morning, and I told him of Mom's disorientation during the night. He was concerned, and asked why I hadn't told him what was happening when he'd awoken and asked about the baseball game. I told him I didn't see any need to concern him at that point. Mom was still sleeping, and Sharon from hospice was on her way over shortly. I told Dad I had to get something out of the car, and slipped outside to call Keira on my cell phone. I told her what had happened, and asked her if she could come back from Cleveland. She immediately started berating herself for having left the previous night, but I told her there was no way we could have known that things were suddenly going to get so weird. She told me she was on her way. I thought about calling Melissa and Caitlin, but decided to wait until I knew more about the situation.

When I went back inside, I casually mentioned to Dad that I had spoken to Keira, and she was on her way in. He started to protest, then stopped, and just nodded his head.

Sharon arrived shortly thereafter, and went in to see Mom. Clearly Mom was glad to see her, and we let Sharon examine her in private as Dad and I sat anxiously in the other room. I glanced over at the coffee table, and noticed an envelope partially concealed by some magazines. I pulled it out, and saw it was a "Peanuts" birthday card, featuring everyone's favorite Beagle, Snoopy. Snoopy cards had always been big in our family, ever since we'd had Breezy.

There was nothing written in the card. Evidently Mom had bought it for me, and hadn't had the chance to fill it out.

Sharon came out into the family room to speak with us. The news was as bad as we'd feared yet expected. She explained that basically, this was Mom's body succumbing to the cancer. Mom's increasing episodes of bewilderment were a natural by-product of her physical decline. It was Sharon's belief that we'd continue to see Mom getting confused, but that she would have many moments of lucidity as well. While naturally Sharon couldn't give an exact time, her best professional guess was that it was a matter of days before Mom would pass away. The most we could do at this point was make Mom as comfortable as possible. She explained how to dispense various pills and drops, including morphine, to keep Mom from suffering. "Can I take the morphine, too?" I joked ruefully. Sharon walked over and hugged me. She hugged my dad, too, which caught him by surprise.

He looked away tearfully, then said, "We'll do whatever we need to."

"That's right, Dad, we will," I said softly.

Sharon went on to tell us that from now on, Mom would be basically bedridden. Her organs were beginning to shut down, and she'd been fitted with a catheter. Sharon showed us how to empty the urine bag, and how to replace it. She also told us how Mom would need to defecate into a diaper at this point, and that we or the nurses could change it whenever necessary. Sharon herself began to tear up, then steadied herself.

"I'll be by every day, and of course, call me anytime. Also, our nurse's aide, Murph, will be coming over every day to give Margaret a bath, clean her up, wash her hair, just make her feel better."

We thanked Sharon for everything, and she left. Dad and I made our way into the bedroom, where Mom was looking at us a bit glassy-eyed.

"How are you feeling, Mom?"

"Well, I've been better, Eddie."

We all sat quietly for a moment, then Mom said, "And a fun time was had by all."

Keira arrived at the Friendship Residence later that evening. She had tears in her eyes the moment she entered the apartment. She asked about Caitlin, and I told her Coll was due to arrive in Pittsburgh tomorrow. Melissa was going to stop in after work. We decided we'd take turns staying on the couch each night, to supervise Mom. The "death watch" had officially begun.

The next day, I helped Dad into the car, loaded his walker into the trunk, and drove us to Beinhauers funeral home. With Mom's demise coming at any moment, we wanted to make sure all the final arrangements were taken care of. I couldn't help but notice the irony that Beinhauers was practically next door to the furniture store where Caitlin and I had purchased

Mom's chair. And just another hundred yards or so up the road was the mausoleum where Dad and Mom had their plots. It was bizarre, as if that lone stretch of road represented the three deteriorating stages of the final days of Mom's life: furniture store, funeral home, mausoleum. One, two, three strikes, you're out.

In his usual efficient manner, Dad had already pre-paid for his and Mom's funeral. We only needed to figure out some details, such as what type of service we wanted to have for her, placing of obituaries in local papers, etc. One item we still had to take care of was choosing the casket.

Like most guys, Dad and I couldn't stand shopping to begin with, but under these circumstances, it was especially untenable. We were greatly aided, however, by the man working with us, Scott Beinhauer. He said he was thirty-five, but looked much younger than his age, which I attributed to his being around all that embalming fluid. His great grandfather had started the family business, and it had been handed down from generation to generation. I guess keeping the business in the family was certainly one way to save on funeral expenses as those generations passed. Scott was a nice, cheerful guy, and as we signed various papers, he talked about the new baby he and his wife had just had, their first. One couldn't help but be struck by the dichotomy of a young man with an infant child, who supports his family by burying dead people. I'll bet his kid will be popular with his classmates on 'Tell us about your dad's job' day. "Go ahead, Pop! Show 'em how you replace the eyeballs with marbles for the viewing!"

Scott took us down the main hallway. I looked around at the décor, which was extremely tasteful.

"You know, Scott, this is really a pretty place for a... well, you know." He smiled. "For a funeral home? Yes, I know. Thank you."

We went into a large room which was stocked with nothing but caskets, and we chose one that was unpretentious, classy, and dignified, just like Mom.

As Scott filled out the paperwork, Dad turned to me and said, "When I die, I want the same casket, Big Ed."
"Well, Dad, I think you should get yourself a separate one. It's a little small for two people." Dad laughed in spite of himself. "Smart ass," he mumbled, then actually tousled my hair. This caught me off guard. He hadn't done that since I was a small, small child. For some reason, this suddenly made the whole situation, us shopping for my mother's coffin, hit me like the terrifyingly sad thing it was. Neither of us said a word during the drive back to the Friendship Residence.

****

Robert and Caitlin arrived from New York the next day. Mom had been in and

out of consciousness during the last thirty-six hours or so. Sometimes she was lucid, sometimes not, but usually somewhere in between. At one point, Melissa was sitting by Mom's bed talking to her, and I walked in and asked Mom if I could bring her something to eat. She looked at me for a moment, then said, "Oh, have you met my daughter Melissa?" Melissa and I looked at each other, and didn't know whether to laugh, or cry, or both. Then, Mom laughed, and said, "Oh, no, of course you've met, being brother and sister. So, your old mom's talking crazy again, isn't she?"
I kneeled down by her bed. "No crazier than usual, Mom," I whispered, and she laughed softly, and when I stroked her hair, she fell asleep almost instantly.

Everyone at the Friendship Residence was concerned for Mom, and though we appreciated it, it started turning into an endless parade of well-meaning but sometimes rather insensitive people traipsing into Mom's room. Honestly, all that was missing was some Shriners driving little cars. At one point, while Murph was giving Mom a sponge bath, Carly, who was one of the owners of the Residence, actually barged right in and entered Mom's room without asking. I had to ask Carly not to do that ever again, and found it pretty amazing that I'd even have to make such a request. I started thinking, gosh, do I have to ask Carly not to do other inappropriate things as well? "Hey, Carly, can you make sure you don't set up a five-piece polka band in my mom's room? Thanks so much!"

This was too much chaos for all of us to bear. We finally had to put a sign on the apartment door asking that people not disturb us. We were *already* disturbed, in many different ways!

Word then came to us that Walter, the man who'd been getting chemotherapy at the same doctor's office as Mom, had passed away during the night. He was such a sweet man, and we all felt terrible upon hearing the news. Even though Mom was unconscious, we thought maybe we should try to tell her, then decided not to. Unfortunately, she'd know soon enough.

Adding to the surreal circumstances was the fact that Halloween was approaching in just a couple days. This meant we got to see images of tombstones, skeletons, and ghosts everywhere we looked. Oh well, I guess one can never be disconcerted enough.

★★★★★★★★★★★★

October 31, 2002. Halloween. It was about 3 PM, and I sat next to Mom's bed as her breathing became more and more labored. She hadn't been conscious in about forty-eight hours. Sharon was in the other room, talking to Dad and my sisters, trying to prepare them for the end. It seemed to be only a matter of hours at this point. I kept rolling the thoughts over and over in my head. Wow, this is it. Mom is going to die on October 31, 2002. That's the day. A day that will never be the same for anybody in our family. It's so strange what one particular square on the calendar can mean to people, what emotions it can conjure up at its mere mention: December 7, September 11, November 22. Now, for me and my family, October 31 would take its place in this pantheon of sorrowful commemoration.

Keira came into the bedroom, and sat on the other side of Mom. We both tried to talk, but found we couldn't. Sharon came in and checked Mom's pulse. We heard a knock on the door, and Caitlin answered to find Father Richmond, our parish priest. We all knew why he was there.

Keira and I stayed in the bedroom, and Caitlin and Robert wandered in. They sat by the bed, and Melissa tip-toed in behind them, not able to glance at Mom for more than a few seconds before tearfully averting her gaze.

Father Richmond, a kindly, cherubic-faced man in his sixties, was set to retire soon from active duty at the church. He was struggling with his own ordeal, a case of diabetes that had already taken part of his foot. He relied on a cane to steady his gait as he entered the bedroom. He spoke briefly to us, and I did my best to carry the family's end of the conversation, as I choked on my words. Father softly mentioned that we should bring Dad in now, and Keira went into the family room to get him.

At this point, we had all surrounded Mom's bed. I was at the foot of the bed, holding, appropriately, Mom's foot. Melissa sat on one side, holding Mom's left arm, and Caitlin and Robert stood on the other side, holding Mom's right. Father stood at the head of the bed, and Sharon stood off to the side, not wanting to be intrusive, but needing to keep an eye on the situation.

Next Keira came into the room, leading my unsteady father, who pushed himself along on his walker. When Dad looked down at Mom, his whole body began to shake, and tears began to stream down his face. He was there to watch his best friend of the last fifty-seven years pass away, right before his eyes.

Dad sat down next to Mom, and spoke softly to her. "I love you, Momma," he choked out.

Father Richmond began to pray aloud, and as I took it all in, I still couldn't believe it was happening. A bunch of people standing around a bed as somebody died, a priest giving last rites...this only happened in movies, right? This had to be the scene of some sad movie I somehow had ended up working on because of some scheduling error. Excuse me, there's been some kind of mistake here! I only do comedies! What's all this sadness? Somebody yell cut, please!

At exactly 4:20 PM, Margaret Driscoll breathed her last breath on this earth, and peacefully expired as her entire family held her. Dad kissed Mom on the forehead and whispered, "See you soon, sweetheart."

****

On a beautiful sunny Saturday afternoon, Mom was put to rest in the Mausoleum. As we stood in front of her plot, I looked around at all the other names that were entombed there. One poor young girl had died at the age of twenty-three, and her picture, which appeared to be from a high school yearbook, adorned her grave. I was filled with compassion for her parents, and all her family, and her friends. It was hard enough on us with our mother passing at age eighty. I could only imagine the level of grief surrounding such a young person's death.

As I turned around to scan the row of tombs directly across from that of my parents, I let out a sudden, loud gasp. Everyone turned to look at me, and I pointed at a grave. It was that of Walter, Mom's fellow chemo patient and friend from the residence. We had no idea he was even in the same cemetery, let alone ten feet from my parents' plots. I felt a quick chill, but oddly, it was a *good* chill.

We all went to lunch at one of Mom's favorite restaurants, and toasted a life well-lived.
"What do you think Mom is doing right now?" Melissa asked wistfully.
"Probably pointing out a spot or two on the pearly gates that need a little dusting." We laughed at the thought of Mom helping keep heaven tidy. Afterward, we went back to the Friendship Residence and watched the Ohio State game, and we smiled thinking about Mom looking down on us and laughing at how excited we were getting during the game. "Mom would have been glad we had the service in the morning. She wouldn't have wanted us to miss kick off," I said, and Dad smiled and nodded in agreement.

CHAPTER FIVE

"Not a bad turnout," Ahmos remarked as I scanned the guests in my house. He was right, there were quite a few people milling about, and some were even playing foosball and the other arcade games I had in my game room. Gosh, it was almost like the "game nights" that were a staple of my existence when I lived in Pittsburgh. A group of us would gather at a different house every Friday night and play a bunch of board games, and who won and who lost was completely secondary to who razzed whom the best. I'd never had that kind of party in LA. I guess I could have tried, but it just seemed like something that wouldn't be "appropriate" in this fast-lane town. Any time I'd had people over, it was in conjunction with some entertainment business event, and the vibe was always more schmoozy than one of sincere enjoyment.

I'd really not even wanted to have this party, but I'd scheduled it months earlier, and it was in honor of the promotion of one of my agents at Endeavor, so I felt obligated to go through with it. It was kind of nice how people seemed to be a little more laid back, not "working the room" as hard as they usually did. However, I couldn't help but notice that several of my Hollywood "friends" not only didn't come, but didn't even bother to tell me they wouldn't be attending. I guess they'd heard the rumors of my impending self-imposed exile from the business, so there was really no reason to invest time in me.

"Man, these are some nice baskets," Ahmos remarked, gesturing at several sympathy gifts that were sent to me following Mom's death.

"Yeah, nothing takes the edge off losing your mother like a box of pears from Harry & David's," I answered. Ahmos gave me a look.

"No, they are nice, it's a nice thing. I appreciate it," I said quietly.

"You sound like you're trying to convince yourself of that," Ahmos replied.

I shrugged. "Isn't it amazing how many people I invited aren't here?"

"Yeah, I'm surprised at some of them, not calling you at the least. But why concentrate on who's not here? Just focus on who is. There's a lot of powerful agents here."

"You're right," I conceded. "I'd better make sure all my valuables are locked up tight."

The next day, I got a call from an LA realtor. Not mine, but somebody representing some potential buyers.

"Hello, Mr. Driscoll, this is Ace Henson of Ace Henson Real Estate."

"Wow, that's quite a coincidence that you have the same name as the guy who owns the company. What are the odds?" I joked.

"I *am* the guy who owns the company," he replied stoically.

"I figured that, I was just kidding. So, how can I help you?"

"I'd like to bring some clients by to see your house sometime today if I could."

"Sure."

"Can you make sure your trash cans aren't outside your house when we come by?"

I made another attempt at humor. "Well, it is trash day, do you think your clients would mind emptying the cans for me?"

"No, I can't ask them to do that!" he replied incredulously. Honestly, if I'd lived in this neighborhood before I became a comedian, I'd never have gone into the business. Undaunted, I plowed ahead. "Why would they be upset to see trash cans out front?"

"Well, it doesn't really help the curb appeal."

"But isn't it actually a *good* sign to have trash cans? Otherwise, it could mean I just keep all the trash piled up *inside* the house."

Ace said nothing, so I gave up. "Okay, Ace, I'll move them myself."

"Will you be home today?"

"Why, are you planning on robbing me?"

Total silence. Hmm, maybe it wasn't too late for me to apply to law school.

"Yes Ace, I'll be home, but I'll hang out in the guest house so I don't bother you kids. But no alcohol or people who don't go to your school, okay?"

The now fully expected silence ensued, and I continued, "I'm sorry, Ace. Listen, I'll make sure everything looks good. I'm anxious to start getting some serious offers on the place."

"Great, we'll see you shortly, Mr. Driscoll."

I hung up and went outside to hide those trash cans, just so prospective buyers would never suspect that LA has a sanitation department. Surely that's a deal-killer.

As I walked to the curb, I briefly entertained the fantasy of putting my trash cans in front of Henrietta's house. Why not? After all, she said no *cars* are allowed, she never said anything about huge, olive-

207

green trash barrels. Luckily I was able to resist such a juvenile notion. Being actively involved in a twelve-step program, I've learned that in many ways, my sobriety rests upon doing the right thing, even under difficult circumstances. I try hard every day to be a good person. Plus, the old bag had security cameras, and she'd have just loved ratting me out to the cops.

As I reached the barrels, I discovered that they'd all been emptied. Excellent, for once the garbage had been collected early in the day. Usually, our street seemed to be the last one in the city to have its trash picked up, which meant that at least one day a week, we could lay claim to having the ripest street in LA. That's no small achievement.

As I grabbed the handle of the first barrel, I noticed that there appeared to be writing on top of the lid. I examined it more closely, and sure enough, written in black sharpie were the words, *"Do not place cans within three feet of parked cars!!"*

What the hell was this about? Who wrote this? I didn't think it was my crazy neighbor, because it was nowhere near her property. It appeared as though it must have been written by the trash guy himself. This was incredible, even by our city's standards. I marched inside and got on the phone to the sanitation department. After being transferred around more times than a pedophile priest, I finally got someone who identified himself as the 'big cahuna."

"What do you need?" asked the cahuna, with a trace of irritation.

"Well, I just went to pull in my trash cans and apparently the driver of the garbage truck wrote a message to me---on the lids!"

"How nice. What did he write?"

"'Do not place cans within three feet of parked cars.'"

"Well, did you?" he inquired in an accusatory tone.

"First of all, when I put the cans out last night, there was nobody parked near them.

Obviously someone parked there after I'd placed them."

"Well, there you go."

I paused for a moment in puzzlement.

"There I go? There I go doing what?"

"Well, some car must have been within the three feet limit."

"But it wasn't *my* car! And I can't control it if someone comes and parks too close to my barrels after I've put them out! What am I supposed to do, sit on my front porch all day cradling a shotgun loaded with buck salt to make sure nobody violates the LA trash demilitarized zone? And why not write a note on the car that's actually parked there, instead of defacing *my* property?"

"Well, I guess our guys didn't know the situation."

"Well, if they were truly offended by my renegade trash can formation, they could have written a note to me on a piece of paper. Maybe stationary with little honey bears on it."

"What?"

"Nothing. Listen, I'm not trying to be rude," I continued. "I just don't appreciate being scolded in permanent marker for something that's not my fault."

"Okay, fine," he barked. "Leave your cans out, and we'll come by later and give you new ones."

I thanked him, and he gave me a grudging "Sure" and hung up.

I sat in my guest house doing some work, waiting for the realtor to ring the doorbell. After several hours had passed, my phone rang.

"Mr. Driscoll? It's Ace Henson."

"Yes, hi Ace. Is everything okay? I thought you were coming by."

"Well, we did come by. But when my clients saw the garbage cans out front, they didn't want to come in."

"Oh, well, I had this uh, thing," I stammered. "I had to leave them out because they're coming to replace---"

"Everybody else on your street seemed to have pulled their barrels in already."

"Yes, I tried to, but they wrote on it, and they're supposed to come and give me new ones---"

"Who wrote on what?" Ace asked.

"Never mind, I'll go pull them in right now."

"That's okay, we went by another place right up the street from you that turned out to be for sale, and my clients loved it and put in an offer. Sorry."

Great. Somebody's car offends a sensitive trash collector, and it costs me the opportunity to sell my house. Seems reasonable. Oh well, I could look at the bright side. At least I'd made my point with the city, and was getting some new trash barrels out of the deal. It was a small victory, but a victory nonetheless.

Early the next morning, I heard the sound of a truck in front of my house, and peered out the window to see that my old cans had been taken and the new ones finally delivered. I sprang out of bed and went out to collect my bounty. I saw that the cans were indeed brand spanking new. And on the lid of each one, written in permanent ink: *"Warning: Keep three feet from all vehicles."*

✱✱✱✱✱✱✱✱✱✱✱✱

I sat in front of my computer, staring forlornly at the words on the screen. They just weren't working. Oh, they were spelled correctly, and they seemed to make sense on the surface, but there was something missing. Actually, several things were missing, such as feeling, and purpose. The same things that more and more seemed to be missing from my life.

I got up and paced around my office, looking out at my backyard, hoping that my too infrequent visitor named "inspiration" might drop by. Why was this so difficult to write? I looked at the screen again. Ugh, it's not very funny, or moving, or anything.

Plus, my deadline was fast approaching, only a week away. Maybe I should go back to that script I'd just finished for Warner Bros. and tweak it up. It had to be easier than writing this damn eulogy.

It had been a tough few days since I'd landed back in LA. For the last week, I'd walked past the chess set in my living room constantly, peeking out of the corner of my eye to see if a piece had moved. But all the chessboard warriors remained in their starting positions.

Back before Mom had passed and I'd asked her about moving a chess piece, I often thought of how frightened I'd be to actually see that a piece had been moved. I thought of how freaked out I'd feel. But since Mom had passed, all I could think of was how happy I'd be, and not scared in the slightest. Honestly, all those books and TV shows about ghosts and apparitions and so forth had always creeped me out in the past. But now, the idea of my mother visiting me, in any form, was something I desperately longed for, and I couldn't imagine it being anything other than completely comforting and exhilarating.

I just couldn't quite get my head around the fact that Mom wasn't here anymore. But where was she? I mean, I believed she was in heaven and all, but what made it so frustrating was the total lack of communication. I didn't expect her to appear to me, though that would be great. But if she could just drop me a letter, or a postcard, telling me everything's okay, that would be perfect. *"Greetings From Paradise, wish you were here...eventually."* Something like that. I just wanted to talk to her again, but I wasn't even that greedy. If she could just leave a message on my answering machine, I'd be quite satisfied. It seemed patently unfair for there to be no communication at all.

Just then, the phone jangled, doing the same to my nerves, and I nearly jumped through the ceiling. It was Ahmos checking in on me.

"How's it going, Ed?"

"Okay, I guess. I'm trying to write this eulogy, and actually make it funny, because I know Mom would want that. But it's a fine line to walk. Maybe I should do it like a George Carlin type of thing, you know, 'Why do they call it a 'service?' I don't see any waiters, who's being 'served' here?'

"You should stick to your own style, Ed," Ahmos commented.

"You're right. Hey, I'm thinking of testing out the material by dropping in on some of the local funeral homes and performing some "guest eulogies."

"Wow, you are a pro. I guess the Comedy Store wouldn't be a good place to do that, huh?"

"I don't think so, although there were certain nights it seemed like a wake." Ahmos laughed. "You're being too hard on yourself. That's *my* job."

"Sorry, I forgot. Still, I may drop by on 'open casket night,' just to try out the jokes."

My friend and fellow comedy writer Jon Macks called shortly thereafter, and I made the same comment about "open casket night" to him. He laughed, and asked if he could include that quote in his new book "How to Be Funny." It was composed of interviews with various comedians and writers, giving advice on humor. He had interviewed a lot of great people, including Garry Shandling, Billy Crystal, Jay Leno, and others, and I told him I was certainly honored to be included.

"Okay, great, I appreciate that," Jon said. "And I'm sorry again for your loss, Eddie."

I was startled. "Why did you call me 'Eddie'?" I asked.

"Gee, I don't know. Don't I call you that sometimes?"

"Not that I remember."

"Hey, I didn't mean to insult you. Is it okay to call you 'Eddie'?"

"It's okay with me, just don't do it in front of any SAG people."

After we'd hung up, I still felt a little weird. Honestly, I don't remember Jon ever referring to me as "Eddie." The only people who call me that are my sisters. And Mom. Well, she used to call me that. Clearly she didn't anymore.

Since both Mom and Chester had passed, I'd started reading a ton of books about spirituality, and the meaning of life. It's exactly what I had done years earlier when Rita had broken off our engagement, and I suddenly had felt lost at sea. This time was worse, though, because I didn't have my mom or chess-playing advisor Chester to lean on.

A friend recommended the book "Talking to Heaven" by James Van Praagh. Though I was skeptical about a guy who claimed to chat with dead folks on a regular basis, I determined to keep an open mind about everything. If there was some way to communicate with Mom, I wanted to find it, not only for me, but for my sisters and especially my dad.

I was calling Dad every day now, to check in and see how he was doing. For the last few years, whenever I'd called Mom and Dad several days in a row, Dad would say, "We appreciate it, Big Ed, but you don't have to call every day. I know you're busy." I couldn't help but notice that though I was calling every day, he'd stopped telling me that I didn't have to do so.

Dad did his best to remain brave, but there was a tone of sadness in his voice that I'd never heard before. I was worried that he would give up on life. Shortly after Mom's funeral, I'd gathered my sisters together to warn them that it was quite common for one spouse to die soon after the other did. I wasn't trying to be unnecessarily gloomy, but I wanted to brace everyone for the distinct possibility of this terrible year getting even worse.

I made a heartfelt plea on the phone to Dad, on behalf of all us kids. "Things are so tough with Mom not around anymore, and it must be especially so for you, Dad. But I hope you know there's still a lot of great life ahead of you, and Mom would want you to live it to its fullest. Plus, I need my dad around, you know?"

There was a long pause, then he quietly said, "Thanks."

"Okay, well, I'll see you next week for the service, Dad."

The next morning, the phone rang while I was still in bed. I glanced at the clock. 5 AM? Man, these telemarketers were really getting ballsy.

I groggily fumbled the receiver as I picked it up, and heard Melissa's voice. Suddenly, I was as awake as I'd have been if someone had thrown the contents of an aquarium in my face. Dad was in the hospital. He'd had a stroke.

Melissa picked me up at the airport in Pittsburgh. She gave me the latest info on Dad, which was surprisingly good. The stroke had been labeled a "mild" one, which seemed odd to me. "Mild" is salsa that doesn't burn your ass the following day. There's nothing "mild" about brain stem trauma. But regardless of semantics, I was glad he was doing better than we'd expected. But now it really didn't seem right anymore for me to be living all the way across the country, so I determined it was time to accelerate my timetable for moving back to Pittsburgh. It was obvious I needed to be home for my family's sake. My sisters shouldn't have to bear the brunt of everything just because they were thoughtful enough to stay in the area. I almost told Melissa on the spot that I was coming back for good, but because I wasn't in the mood for the "you have to stay in LA" speech that she'd inevitably give me, I silently determined that I'd talk to her about it at some later time.

We drove straight to the hospital, and as I walked down the corridor to his room, I was happy to hear Dad feistily complaining about his dinner being cold. I stuck my head through the doorway.

"Hello, I'm the maître d'. Is there a problem here, sir?"

Dad looked up with a smirk. "Yes, actually there is. Your restaurant is lousy!"

"Of course it is," I continued. "Don't you see, that's why we have all these doctors and nurses around, because our food makes people sick."

The nurse looked up at me and smiled. "I'll warm this up for you, Mr. Driscoll," she told Dad, then winked at me as she left. Melissa excused herself to check on some of the insurance papers at the front desk.

Just then, my cell phone rang. I thought I'd turned it off, because I knew hospitals generally don't permit their use. Dad gave me a bemused look. "Well, that must be you, Mr. Hollywood, because I don't have a cell phone." I saw on the caller ID that it was Ahmos, and I answered.

"Hey, I'm at the hospital," I whispered. "You should call me later, I don't want the signal from this call to be responsible for cutting off some guy's respirator or something."

"Oh, sorry. How's your dad?"

"Pretty good, I'm here with him now. Ahmos says 'hi" Dad."

Dad smiled and said, "Tell him thanks."

Ahmos continued, "Listen, I can call you later, but I just wanted to let you know that the Comedy Store wants to extend your show run."

I stepped away from Dad. "Absolutely not!" I snapped. "I won't be extending my show, because that will extend my time away from here. My family needs me."

"Well, of course, you don't have to extend it right away, you can take some weeks off until everything's okay back there."

"The only way everything will be okay back here is if / am back here. So please tell them thank you very much, but there will

223

be no extending my show. I'm looking forward to finishing the run as agreed when I get back to LA."

I suddenly realized I was louder than I meant to be, and looked over to see Dad staring at me.

"Listen, we'll talk later," I whispered into the phone, and flipped it shut.

I walked back over to the side of Dad's bed. "Sorry, just some business stuff."

"Big Ed, the room's not that large. I could hear you. I hope you're not seriously thinking of moving back here."

I looked down for a moment, then back up into his eyes. "Dad, would you really be upset to see me more often?"

"You know that's not what I'm saying, son."

"Then what *are* you saying?" I asked, my voice starting to choke up with emotion.

"Big Ed, what's bothering you?"

"Besides my mom being gone and my dad in the hospital?" I blurted out.

"Yes, besides all that," Dad replied firmly.

"I don't know how to put it all in words, Dad. And I realize the irony of that statement given my occupation." I cleared my throat and continued.

"I hate being so far away from you and the rest of the family. And my best friends. And so far from Mom's grave..." My voice cracked, and I stopped.

"I understand that, Big Ed. We all miss you, too. But that's just part of doing your work. Your job requires you to be in a city that happens to be far away from your roots. It's part of the tradeoff that people make every day in order to pursue their destiny. You've always seemed like you adjusted to being out West pretty damn well, as far as I can see."

"Well, California is certainly not the worst place in the world, but...I don't know, Dad. The average person outside of LA views Hollywood as this magical place, and I guess that's Hollywood's job, making everything appear magical. But when you're smack in the middle of it all, the whole Hollywood machine is a far different experience that what others might imagine it to be."

Dad listened carefully to my words, then said, "I understand how you're feeling, Ed, but you're doing amazing stuff. You're living out your childhood dream, you've been amazingly successful."

"And I'm incredibly grateful for that, and I think you know that. It's just that for the last few years, I've really started to question just what the hell I'm doing out there. Not that things in this world usually make sense to me, but at the moment they seem to make even less sense than usual."

"Big Ed, you know I like to tease you about being "Mr. Show Biz," but I hope you realize that in reality, I very much respect what you do. It's important."

"Making jokes? How is that important? Over the last few months, I've seen doctors and nurses and all sorts of people making a real difference in people's lives, right when they need it most. I'm supposed to put myself in that category because I make fun of airplane food and bad TV commercials?" Dad smiled, and motioned me to sit down in the chair by his bed.

"You know, when I was working for U.S. Steel in Cleveland, your mother and I were very happy. We loved the neighborhood we were in, I liked all the people I worked with, things seemed pretty, well, almost perfect. Then, I was rather suddenly transferred to Pittsburgh, to a whole new department in a whole new office where I didn't know anybody. And of course, your sisters and your mom were not too excited about leaving a city they'd become very fond of. And neither was I, but I knew I had to do it. I knew it was the best thing for everyone involved."

Dad removed his glasses and rubbed his forehead, as though he was summoning all the emotions of that time so many years ago.

"Well, of course, we moved to Pittsburgh. Soon after, your mother became pregnant

227

with our first and only boy. And we moved into the best neighborhood we'd ever been a part of. And the people I worked with in the metallurgy department are still my closest friends to this very day. Those that are alive, anyway," he added with a wry grin.

"Dad, I'm not sure why you're telling me this," I said.

Dad put his glasses back on and looked at me. "I've been around a few years more than you, son. And I may not know much, but I do believe that life is always pointing each of us in the right direction, telling us what to do. It may not even be what you *want* to do, but it's what circumstances dictate that you *should* do. *We're* the ones who choose to either do what life's showing us to, or to resist it and be unhappy."

"Well, I agree, Dad. And right now, it would be pretty easy to conclude that life is clearly signaling me to come back home."

Dad mulled this comment for a few seconds, then said, "It's not always easy to read the signals properly. A pretty wise man once said to me, 'Mom would want you to live your life to the fullest.'"

We sat in silence for a few minutes, then Melissa returned with the nurse trailing just behind her. Soon Dad's room was overflowing with people. Keira came in, and Caitlin and Robert arrived from Saratoga shortly thereafter. Mom's memorial mass was in just two days, and we were all concerned about Dad being able to attend. I raised the idea of postponing the mass, but Dad would have none of it. He insisted he'd be there. It was fine to have Dad's okay, but as far as the rest of the family was concerned, we were much more interested in getting the doctor's approval.

Happily, Dr. Montini felt that if Dad's condition improved, or even stayed the same, he'd be fine to go to the mass, though he would absolutely have to be in a wheelchair. Dad wasn't strong enough to use his walker. I knew Dad would probably argue briefly with that part, but also knew we could make him understand that it was the only way.

Visiting hours ended, and we went our separate ways. Melissa dropped me off at Turk and Ann's place, and I knocked on their front door. Their oldest daughter, Lisa, who was ten, swung open the door, shouted, "Uncle Ed!" and gave me a huge bearhug. She said nothing else, just squeezed me tight. I knew that she knew what was going on with me, though I wasn't sure quite how her parents had explained it all. I didn't understand it at forty, so how could she get her mind around it at her age? But she knew I was hurting, and with wisdom belying her age, she was doing her part to let me know I was loved. The rest of the family emerged from the house, and threw themselves on me in the type of group hug you usually only see in movies. "Okay, okay, get off me, people. I know you're just trying to distract me while Turk swipes my wallet."

"Shit, you figured out our plan!" said Turk.

"Mommy, he said the 's' word!" the kids gleefully pointed out.

"Yes, he did, didn't he?" I agreed. "Don't you think Daddy should be punished?"

The kids screamed their agreement.

"Having Uncle Ed here is my punishment," shot back Turk.

After the kids had gone to bed, us "grown-ups" sat staring at the fireplace. Turk and Ann still had both their parents, and shook their heads trying to imagine the unimaginable.

"I feel bad about you having to go through this alone, Ed," said Ann, then suddenly caught herself. "Of course, you're not alone, you have me and Turk and your sisters and..."

I told her it was okay, I knew what she was saying. Yeah, it was sort of hard not having a significant other to help me through all this. But I realized that Rita wouldn't have been the right person, and for that matter, neither would Heather. Would it be great to have the right woman with me through all this? Absolutely, but it would be worse to have the wrong woman. Who knows, maybe I was supposed to deal with all this without a wife or girlfriend, in order to be able to take care of my family. I wasn't sure what the reason was, or even if there *was* one, but no matter what, this was the way it was. Whether it was truly "God's plan" or just a random act of fate, I had to do as best as I could with the cards that were dealt me.

I mentioned that I was reading the Van Praagh book, and Ann told me he hosted a TV program that she watched regularly. In fact, she had recorded a lot of episodes, and she flipped on the television to show me. I was surprised when I heard Van Praagh speak. As I'd been reading his book, the voice in my head was one of dulcimer tones, a sort of booming, confident, God-like voice, befitting a spiritual medium. The one I heard on TV was surprisingly high-pitched, almost cartoony.

At first I thought he was channeling Mel Blanc or something. Nope, that was his real voice alright.

I wasn't sure if I fully believed that he was legit, but I wanted to keep an open mind. I enjoyed watching the show, and he seemed pretty sincere. I noticed that the show was taped in LA, and made a mental note to look into perhaps attending a taping when I got back to the west coast.

That night, I lay in the guest bedroom, reading Van Praagh, and of course, now hearing that much squeakier voice in my head. Right as I was about to turn in for the night, I read a paragraph that caused me to sit up suddenly. Van Praagh stated that often, people will ask their loved ones to show them a sign, such as moving an object, after they've passed over. He contended this was hard for spirits to do, especially recently deceased ones, because life was mostly energy, and it was easier for spirits to communicate through electricity. He posited that in time, spirits

233

learned to move heavier things. But in the early stages, he suggested it was better to ask a deceased loved one to blink a light.

Even though I wasn't completely sold on Van Praagh's credibility, this new "electricity" information certainly was interesting, especially considering my "chess piece" request. I'd have to give it some thought.

I was finally feeling tired, and Mom's mass was the next day, so I decided I'd better go to sleep. After a few moments of waiting for Mom to do it, I finally reached over and turned off the bedside lamp myself.

The next morning, as Turk, Ann and I sat sipping coffee in their kitchen, I brought up what I'd been reading the night before. "Well, it's interesting reading, all right, but you don't really believe all that stuff about lightbulbs and so forth, do you Ed?" asked Turk.

Before I could answer, Ann interjected.

"Don't make Ed cynical about Van Praagh!" she admonished Turk.

"*Me* make *Ed* cynical?" chuckled Turk. "Ed wrote the book on cynicism."

"Actually, I'm on the second draft of my book about cynicism," I laughed.

Ann grabbed my arm. "Seriously, don't let yourself be too skeptical without giving it all a chance. Don't you think there's a lot of stuff we don't understand in this life?"

"Of course," I answered. "Hey, I can't even figure out how the remote control for your TV works. I had to unplug it last night just to turn it off."

"No wonder I couldn't turn on the TV this morning," said Turk. "I didn't even notice it was unplugged."

"Well, see there?" answered Ann. "There's a lot of things you guys can't figure out, so what gives you the right to scoff at Van Praagh?"

It was hard to argue with her point. We finished up our coffee and headed out to pick up Dad.

We loaded Dad and his wheelchair into Melissa's SUV and headed to St. John's church. We were gratified, and not surprised, by the large number of people who came out to pay their respects. When the time came for me to walk to the podium to deliver Mom's eulogy, I silently prayed for the strength to make it through my little speech without completely losing it.

I walked to the podium, and nervously produced some papers from inside my suit jacket. I'd finally written something up, but it still felt woefully inadequate for such an amazing woman.

I looked out at the attendees, and at my family sitting in the first pew, then folded the papers up and put them back in my pocket.

I decided right then and there to just speak from the heart, or in comedian lingo, "wing it."

I told the story of having suggested to Mom that we have a service *before* she died, then have her walk out and scare the hell out of everyone. The congregation laughed, and I said, "But unless she's got a real surprise for us all, I don't think that will happen today." I glanced behind me, hoping she'd somehow appear for real. But alas, she didn't stroll out from behind the altar, and I continued.

I told several other stories, all humorous in nature, about things Mom had said and done, mostly involving her husband and kids. People smiled and laughed through their tears, me included. I thanked Mom for all she'd done for us, for being one of the two best people I'd ever known, the other being Dad. "Mom always told me that if I keep my eyes and ears and heart open, I can find all I'm ever looking for. She said it had always worked for her." I started to choke up, but plowed ahead.

"It's a sad thing that Mom is gone, because this world needs people like her. But I suppose heaven needs people like her as well, and I'm sure she's busy now making it an even more wonderful place than it had been before her arrival."

Dad smiled and nodded at me, and I realized I'd better wrap it up before I fell apart, or even worse for a performer, started to bore people! I thanked everyone for coming, and invited them to join us for food and drink in the church social hall. "Just mention my name, and you'll get half off the cover charge," I concluded, and swore I could almost hear Mom laughing and saying, "Oh, Eddie!"

Just after the service, a long-time friend of Mom's, Mrs. Angie, approached me. "That was lovely, Ed. Your mother had such a great sense of humor, just like you." She hugged me hard, then excused herself. I wheeled Dad into the social hall, and we began visiting with all the guests.

After we'd eaten and shared stories with all the others at the church, our family drove out to the mausoleum to visit Mom. We all took turns walking up to Mom's grave and speaking to her. I approached and whispered to her that I hoped she wasn't embarrassed by anything I'd said at mass. As usual, I told her how much I loved her and missed her, then, almost as an afterthought, I told her what I'd been reading in the Van Praagh book, and said if it was easier, she could flash some lights or something like that to give me a "shout out." But I still wanted a chess move at some point, I added, before saying goodbye.

We took Dad back to the hospital, and we stayed in his room and watched the Ohio State game, as we knew Mom would want us to do. Of course, it had to be an incredibly tense game that eventually went into overtime. I wasn't sure this was a good thing for someone who'd recently had a stroke!

I was a bit surprised when Caitlin blatantly invoked Mom's name for help as the game got tense in the fourth quarter. "Come on, Mom, help us out up there!" she shrieked. Even I laughed at that one, figuring that though Mom would certainly want to help, there were probably a good number of Illinois fans in heaven, too, and God probably wouldn't want to take sides. Still, I reckoned it couldn't hurt.

At one point, OSU almost turned the ball over, and we all screamed out loud. A nurse came dashing into the room. "Is everything okay?" she asked with a frightened look on her face.
"Um, yeah, just, we almost fumbled," I explained sheepishly. "Sorry, we'll keep it down." She looked at us like we were crazy, and it was hard to argue with that assessment.

Luckily, the Buckeyes won, and I was just thankful it didn't go into double overtime, or I think I would have had to get a room at the hospital for myself.

After saying good-night to Dad, we all went back to Melissa's to unwind. We stayed pretty late, and as I let myself into

Turk's house that night, I did so as quietly as possible so as not to wake anyone. I wearily plodded up to the guestroom, flipped on the light switch, and jumped involuntarily when two separate lightbulbs blew out noisily.

I stood silently in the dark for several minutes, trying to assess what had just occurred. Mom? Coincidence? I shook my head and smiled. Most likely cause? Cheap bulbs!

CHAPTER SIX

"You know, I just want to take a moment to thank you all for being here tonight. And I see a lot of people who have been here several times over the past few months, and to you folks especially, I have to say; what is your problem? I mean, seriously, I have to be here to listen to this crap every week, but you don't...get a life!"

Laughter rolled through the packed room, and I took a moment to soak it all in. "I hate to see a good thing end. And some critics would argue, I obviously hate to see a good thing begin, too." I squinted out at the capacity crowd in front of me. "Thanks for being part of the last show, because without all you people here...I'd be standing here talking to myself, which is what I do the other 23 hours of my day. Good night!" I walked offstage to thunderous applause, with more peace of mind than perhaps I'd ever felt before in my life. Knowing that I'd ended on a good note, and knowing that I'd

242

soon be leaving Hollywood and everything it involves, was a potent combination. I was relieved, tired, and happy with what, all in all, I considered a job well done.

Backstage, Ahmos gave me a hug and told me he was proud of me. While he was generally encouraging after shows, he was more emotional than usual. I think he'd finally come to terms with the fact that I was really leaving LA and show business. Though he was disappointed, I knew he always had my happiness utmost in his mind, something that not many talent managers would feel, let alone understand.

Comedian Pauly Shore, who oversees the Comedy Store, stopped by afterwards to congratulate me.

"Ed, I hope you'll reconsider and extend the show. We'd love to have you," he said, then looked at Ahmos as if wanting him to chime in and convince me. "I've tried, Pauly, believe me," Ahmos said with a wry grin, and I thanked Pauley for his kindness during the course of the run.

243

Everything seemed to finally be falling into place. A Hollywood film company was about to put a deposit down on my LA house, purchasing it for an employee and his family that were relocating from New York, and I had a great lead on a house in Pittsburgh. Though I knew Dad was not going to be very thrilled initially when I told him I was back in Pittsburgh for good, I was confident he'd adjust to it.

★★★★★★★★★★★★

With my move back East now imminent, I realized I was sadly lacking in the most important commodity required for a move: boxes.

I made the mistake of asking a few of my fellow writers if they had any extra boxes, and they all looked at me like I was crazy. "We don't save boxes, Ed. If you need some, go buy them." How Hollywood, I thought. "Buy" boxes? It just didn't seem right. Remember the old days when you'd just go to your neighborhood grocery store and they'd give you boxes for free? Yeah, me neither, but I'm pretty sure that's how it used to be.

Resignedly, I drove to a nearby "packaging" store. Though I was the only customer in the place, the clerk let me stand at the counter for a full thirty seconds while he finished reading an article in "Variety." I started to think he didn't see me, so I spoke up.

"Hello," I offered.

"Be with you in a minute," he replied without looking up.

It soon became evident that with this guy, "a minute" was not a figure of speech, but the actual time he was willing to let me stand there.

"Is there a review of your store in there?" I finally asked, pointing at his copy of "Variety."

He sighed dramatically, slowly put the trade paper down, and for the first time looked right at me.

"What can I do for you?"

"I'd like to buy some boxes, please."

He pointed his thumb to a chart behind the counter and yawned, "There's the prices."

I looked up to see that the boxes were priced from five dollars for shoebox-sized ones, all the way up to fifteen dollars each for cartons that were about three feet by three feet.

"Wow, kind of expensive, huh?" I muttered. The clerk was unmoved. "These are high quality boxes, man."

"I guess so," I replied. "With prices like that, they should be displayed on velvet pillows under glass."

"We don't take checks," he snarled, obviously realizing he had a cheapskate in front of him. You could practically see the thought bubble forming above his head reading, "If you have to ask how much the boxes are, you can't afford them!"

I asked for fifteen boxes of various sizes, and he reached under the counter and produced a completely flat stack of

246

cardboard, plopping it noisily down on the countertop.

"Here you go, pal."

"You mean, I have to assemble them, too?" I asked.

"No, *you* don't have to. But somebody does. Actually, we can build them for you if you'd like."

"Thanks, that would be great. I'm pretty mechanically disinclined," I said sheepishly.

"It's five dollars extra for each box we put together."

"You're kidding," I replied.

The clerk shrugged his shoulders. "That's how it is. You get what you pay for."

"I understand that," I stammered. "But something's wrong when the boxes themselves are more valuable than their contents, don't you think?"

"I don't think," he replied without irony. "I just work here."

I couldn't argue with him on that count. So I maxed out my credit card to complete the order, and stacked the flat, "high quality"

boxes in the back of my car. The clerk
didn't offer to help, and I sure wasn't going
to ask him. I could only imagine the fee for
actually loading the boxes. I headed home
to spend the rest of the day, if not the
entire week, assembling them.

That night, as I sat on my living room
floor, surrounded by scattered mounds of
cardboard, my phone rang.

"Boxes R Us," I answered on a whim.

"Ed?" came the confused voice of Ahmos.

"Yeah, it's me. I'm trying to organize some
of my stuff for the move, but these boxes I
bought aren't cooperating."

"You *bought*?"

"Yeah."

"We have tons of empty boxes here at the
office that we throw out every day. Why
didn't you just ask me?"

"Because I'm a moron," I sighed.

"Apparently my head is emptier than your
boxes."

"Not to add to your obviously difficult day," Ahmos segued. "But you might want to wait a bit before you start packing."
This didn't sound good.
"Remember that show you did for Warner Brothers last year?" he asked.
"Sure. I don't think viewers remember it, but I do."
"Well, apparently more viewers recollect it than you might have thought. The show has just been picked up again."
"Well, that's good. I liked the people I worked with."
"That's a good thing, Ed, because you'll be working with them again."
"Only if they've decided to start filming in Pittsburgh," I said defensively.
"Um, here's the thing you may not remember. Your contract called for you to continue on the show if it's picked up."
Yes, it was all coming back to me now.
"Well, can't we get out of it?" I asked, sounding like a teenager trying to avoid cutting the lawn.

"Not really, Ed, at least not without a lot of legal problems. But here's the thing, you also gave them your word, remember?" Damn, he was right. I had promised the producer I would be there if the show got rolling. This was the clincher. How could I criticize people in Hollywood for not having any values, and at the same time go back on my word? Once again, the sheer inconvenience of doing the right thing had reared its ugly head.

"Yeah, Ahmos, you're right. I have to do it. But it shouldn't hold me up for too long, correct?" I asked hopefully.

"Uh, no," Ahmos demurred. "No longer than...eight months or so."

"Ugh!" I complained. "That's a long time."

"I know."

"Well, there's nothing I can do about it now. And it's not as though Dad is begging me to move back to Pittsburgh anyway. He'd rather I don't, so I guess it's not a big problem to delay things another eight months. But what do I do about the deposit on my house?"

"I'll help you with that. Maybe we can ask the film company to rent your house to you for the last few months you're in town, before they move in their employee."

"So somehow, I've gone from owning my house to hoping to rent it," I summarized.

"Ed, I know you're not happy about having to wait all this time," Ahmos continued.

"It's okay," I declared. "Hell, I'll need the money from the gig anyway if I'm going to pay off these boxes."

And so, for the next eight months, I worked on the television show as I'd promised. The deposit on the house turned out to not be an issue, as the film company didn't want to rent the house back to me, and ended up pulling out of the deal completely. The producers at my TV show were nice enough to give me a few days off here and there so that I could go back to Pittsburgh occasionally to check up on Dad.

251

He had been getting along really well at the Friendship Residence, becoming much more involved socially with the other tenants. We were all proud of how he'd managed to keep his spirits up and moving forward since Mom had passed. One of the guiding reasons for his finding enthusiasm for life again was knowing that Mom would have wanted him to carry on.

Of course, I'd gone home for Christmas, which had certainly been a far more solemn occasion that it ever had been before, but we knew Mom would be glad we were all together in Pittsburgh, as we'd always been every Christmas, no matter what.

And, I'd gone back the first week in January, to bring Dad some souvenirs of Ohio State winning the National Championship in the Fiesta Bowl, which I'd attended. In typical heart-stopping fashion, OSU had won in double overtime. One critical penalty flag had taken an unusually long time for the referee to throw, and in fact was so late, Miami thought they'd won the game, and began celebrating on the field. But the flag finally came out, giving the Buckeyes new life. Melissa speculated that Mom had pulled that flag out of the referee's pocket. It was an incredible ending to an incredible season, a season that seemed to truly be one of destiny. Funny how I easily accepted the premise that sports teams could follow supernaturally determined paths, but couldn't quite believe that was true of individuals' lives.

I'd gone back in February, when Dad had suffered yet another "mini-seizure." Honestly, it seemed like he'd experienced more strokes than an Olympic swimmer at that point, but unsurprisingly to my sisters and me, he'd bounced back in amazing fashion once again.

I'd gone back in March, to spend St. Patrick's Day with him. We listened to Irish music, and Dad got teary-eyed, recalling how much Mom enjoyed decorating the house with shamrocks and other Irish trinkets. Though she was half-Irish herself, she seemed to do it all more out of homage to Dad's one hundred percent Irish ethnicity than to her own lineage.

I hadn't been able to make it back for Dad's birthday on May 1, but that weekend I was at the Pirates-Dodgers game in Dodger Stadium, and I passed a note up to the television booth to long-time Bucco broadcaster Lanny Frattare. I had first met Lanny when I was a senior in high school when he came to speak at a function I attended. Years later, I met up with him again, when I was doing commercials for the Pirates. We'd crossed paths here and there over the years, and thanks to the miracle of satellite TV, I was able to listen to his broadcasts in my house in LA. It was always comforting to hear his voice calling a game in his inimitably smooth, folksy fashion. It gave me fond memories of so many summer nights Dad and I spent listening to his play-by-play.

My note to Lanny on that day in Dodger Stadium invited him to my show that weekend at the Comedy Store, and asked him to pass along happy eighty-fifth birthday wishes to Dad during the broadcast, which Lanny did. Dad and all the other guys at the Friendship Residence heard it, and it made Dad a huge celebrity with everyone. Lanny was nice enough to send me a handwritten note, too, thanking me for the invite to my show. If there's a classier guy out there than Lanny Frattare, I haven't met him.

Now, it was August 2003, and my obligation to the Warner Brothers show was finished. As so often happens, the show got cancelled. And though the film studio had passed on buying my LA house months ago, there were now several serious inquiries, and a deal to sell it appeared to be just around the corner. I felt there really was nothing at this point to keep me from setting the relocation wheels in motion. I still hadn't told Dad that I was coming back for good. I figured I wouldn't tell him until I was literally moving into a house in Pittsburgh. That way, there'd be nothing he could really say against it because it would be too late. I was headed back to Pittsburgh under the guise of attending a baseball game with Dad, and figured while I was there I could finally find a house to buy.

I was excited to take Dad to his first baseball game at PNC Park. Pittsburgh had built its beautiful new venue two years earlier, and back then I told Dad that when Mom got better, we'd all have to go to a game there. But after Mom passed away, Dad resignedly insisted that now, he'd never see a game at PNC. He claimed he didn't have the energy to do what was required. He was using his wheelchair full-time by now, and he didn't seem to understand how handicapped-accessible public places are these days. But I insisted on taking him, because I knew from attending games there just how accommodating the park is, not only the facilities themselves, but the people who worked there.

Dad kept insisting he didn't want to be a bother, and it would be too hard for us to take him to the park. I don't know if it was his own fear, or stubbornness, or some sense of guilt at going to the park without Mom, but he had resisted the idea for quite awhile.

Finally, I told him, "Come on, Dad, believe me, there are physically challenged people at the park every night."

"Yeah, I know," he muttered. "They're called the Pirates starting line-up."

At last, Dad agreed to go, and as the day of the game approached, he seemed more eager to attend. He also was emboldened by the fact that the Friendship Residence had taken a field trip to a theatre downtown to see "Riverdance." The theatre was filled with fellow octogenarians, and Dad was impressed with how easily he had been able to travel to the show, sit in the theatre, and go back home, all without having to leave the comfort of his wheelchair. Quite ironic, if you think about it. Irish dancers not moving from the waist up, with much of their audience not moving from the waist down.

Luckily, my friend Turk did a lot of advertising with the Pirates, and he hooked me up with four tickets right behind home plate. Caitlin and Robert were flying in from Saratoga, and the four of us were going to enjoy the day at PNC.

Ahmos had called me the day after Turk got me the tickets, because he'd received a nice offer from Troy Miller, a brilliant director/producer who wanted me to consult on his new show, for "just a couple days." Though I always loved working with Troy, and was definitely appreciative of the offer, I didn't want to postpone my trip to Pittsburgh, and told Ahmos that I needed to stop taking gigs or I'd never get out of Hollywood. Usually, Ahmos would try to talk me into taking the job, especially one with such upsides to it, but for the first time I can remember, he didn't resist at all. Of course, I could have traded in the tickets for another game a few weeks later and just taken Dad to that one instead, but I just felt that I needed to keep my original plans.

While pacing around the house one evening, ruminating about all the logistics of the upcoming move back home, I wandered into my living room. I stared at my chess sets, and realized I hadn't played in awhile. I noticed that there was actually dust on the boards, and got out a dust cloth to clean them up.

There was something peaceful about cleaning off the boards, so I took the time to wipe all the pieces clean as well. It felt almost as good as actually playing a game, or going through the moves of some old classic match from one of my books.

As I finished dusting the last pawn from the chess-table in my living room, I placed it on its home square and said aloud, "It's your move, Mom."

★★★★★★★★★★★★

"Just let me use the bathroom, Big Ed, before we head out to the game." Caitlin, Robert, and I watched as Dad carefully maneuvered his wheelchair down the hall and into the bathroom. We didn't bother to ask him if he needed any help, because we knew he'd say "no," unless he really, really, required it. He was still struggling to be as self-sufficient as possible, but thankfully, he'd reached a point where he wasn't afraid to ask for a helping hand when he absolutely needed it. I'd often "help" him get into bed, which meant mostly keeping an eye on him as he slowly raised himself out of his wheelchair, then hoisted himself up on his walker, then dropped himself onto the edge of his bed. Then, one leg at a time, he'd take off his trousers, then, one leg at a time, put on his

260

pajamas. He'd repeat the process with his socks, and shoes, and shirt, every night, and every morning. I couldn't help but be touched by how these small, everyday necessities were such a struggle for him at this point, and I marveled at the bravery and uncomplaining fashion in which he completed these daily tasks that most of us take for granted.

I was struck by how hard his life seemed to be now, the sheer energy required to live each day with such pronounced physical disadvantages, and especially to have to do so without his beloved wife. And Dad was one of the lucky ones, in that he had family and friends to care for him, a nice place to live, and great medical care. The thought of all the elderly people who didn't have the financial means to be as comfortable, or those who had no family to care for them, was almost too horrible to contemplate. I'd noticed that some of the people at the Friendship Residence seemed to never have visitors, even during the holidays. I tried to make sure I chatted with them whenever I saw them, even if for just a few minutes. And I was glad that I would soon be back in town for good, and be able to visit far more often.

Dad seemed to age exponentially every time I saw him, even though I saw him nearly every month. It was as though the aging process had kicked into a higher gear since Mom's death. He seemed to fall asleep quite often, no matter what the circumstance.

"You know, Dad," I kidded, "I'll bet you're the only guy around who could fall asleep on the floor of the stock exchange."

Dad laughed, and answered, "I'd rather fall asleep than have to watch my stocks drop."

The game we were to attend seemed tailor-made for Dad. It was a rare Thursday afternoon game, which meant there wouldn't be as many people there, the traffic to and from wouldn't be so bad, and it wouldn't be too late of an evening for him. We all figured he'd probably nod off at some point during the game, but we knew we could leave whenever Dad got too tired. The forecast had mentioned some possible rain, but it was a sunny morning, and there didn't seem to be any storm clouds looming so far.

Robert helped me get Dad's wheelchair out of the trunk, and we loaded him in and rolled him through Gate A at the ballpark, while Caitlin parked the car. Turk had been nice enough to procure us passes to eat lunch in the Season Ticket Holder VIP area, which was decorated with great photos of past and present Pirates, World Series trophies, bats, balls, and gloves from memorable games. We enjoyed a delicious buffet lunch as we reminisced about past games from the Pirates' storied history. We'd always stayed loyal to our team, through the good times and, more recently, the bad.

After lunch, we took the ramp to the elevator to go to our seats. On the way, we passed a wall filled with photographs of the Pirates' previous homes, Forbes Field and Three Rivers Stadium. We talked about the first game Dad brought me to, at Forbes Field, where poor Dad sat in the seat behind one of the ubiquitous pillars that blocked fans' views, so I could sit in the seat with the unobstructed view. Just another in an endless series of sacrifices a good parent makes on behalf of their child. We talked about the first game we'd all attended as a family at Three Rivers Stadium when it opened in 1970. I reminisced about Mom, Keira, and I being at Three Rivers when Roberto Clemente got his three-thousandth and final hit. It was an afternoon game, and Dad couldn't go because he was working. I'm not sure why I wasn't in school, but it's a cherished memory, though bittersweet in light of Clemente being killed in a plane crash just months after that game.

Dad took in all the photos, then commented, "It's sure nice to see all your heroes up there, isn't it, Big Ed?"

"Well, Dad, I'm talking to my *real* hero right now."

He grinned, and we waited for Caitlin and Robert to catch up to us as they slowly perused the memorabilia.

As the ushers guided us to our special wheelchair accessible seats near the Pirates dugout, Dad's eyes widened. The view was breathtaking, not only being so close to the action, but the fact that the outfield of PNC featured an incredible panorama of the city skyline. The US Steel building, where Dad had worked for most of his life, stood prominently above the other buildings that lie across the river, just over the Roberto Clemente bridge.

Dad said they were the best seats he'd ever had, which was somewhat remarkable given that he'd been going to games for over seventy years, and had seen everyone from Babe Ruth to Mickey Mantle to Pete Rose to Barry Bonds. I was so happy I was able to take HIM to a game for once, and get such great seats. I definitely owed Turk big-time for this one.

"Okay, Dad and Eddie, picture time," Caitlin announced, and she took a photo of us with the park and city in the background.

During the game, we kept sneaking looks at Dad to see if he was getting tired, but I hadn't seen him that alert in a long time. He was riveted to every single pitch, offering commentary about what specific type of pitch he guessed was being thrown. By the eighth inning, the skies were starting to darken, and it seemed as though the rain previously predicted was about to make an appearance. The Pirates were down by five runs now, and we thought maybe Dad was getting tired, and asked him if he wanted to leave.

"Hell, no, I don't want to leave! Why, do you guys want to leave?" Dad asked. Caitlin said, "No, not at all, Dad. We just wanted to make sure you were comfortable."

"Well, I'll be a lot more comfortable if we can get some runs here," Dad replied, and we all happily stayed in our seats until the very last out. Unfortunately, the Pirates weren't able to provide those "comfortable" runs, and instead lost quite uncomfortably. But it had been such an enjoyable day that asking for a win almost seemed a bit too avaricious. We made our way back to the car, and just after we loaded Dad and his wheelchair in, raindrops started thudding off the windshield.

"Wow, how about that timing!" exclaimed Dad.

I replied, "Perfect, Dad. Just perfect."

Back at the Residence that night, the four of us had dinner while we watched the thunderstorm through the dining hall windows. Caitlin and Robert were planning to drive back to Saratoga in the morning, and I was set to fly to LA, and we hoped

267

the thunderstorms would be cleared out by then. Dad regaled the other residents with the adventures of the day at PNC, and some of the guys razzed Dad for the Pirates not winning.

"I could have run to first base as fast as some of our players," Dad commented, drawing the laughs of the other diners.

By the next morning, the sunshine had broken through, and Robert, Caitlin, and I had breakfast with Dad. Afterwards, Caitlin and Robert loaded up their car and headed back to upper New York state.

I took a walk over to a house not far from the Friendship Residence. I'd noticed a sign in front reading "For Sale by Owner, Inquire Within Anytime," and thought it might be more efficient to cut out the increasingly flaky middlemen realtors I'd been dealing with. I rang the bell, and almost immediately the door swung open revealing a warmly smiling woman who appeared to be in her seventies.

"Good morning," I said pleasantly.

"Good morning to you, young man," she replied.

'Young man.' I loved this lady already.

"What are you selling, dear?" she asked.

"Actually, I'm hoping to buy. I noticed your house is for sale."

"Please come in, dear." She opened the screen door for me, and I stepped inside the house. She introduced herself as Sophie.

"I've loved living here, but it's way more room than this one lady needs," she said. "I'm going to be moving to Friendship Residence."

"My father lives there, I've just been visiting him. It's a nice place."

"Would you like some tea?" she asked.

Now *this* is how neighbors treat each other in Pittsburgh, I thought. Sophie didn't even seem to mind that I'd parked in front of her house. Imagine that. "No, thank you," I answered. "I actually have to catch a flight later today, but would love to see the rest of the house."

Sophie showed me around, and I was impressed. The word "charming" immediately sprang to mind. The house was immaculate, with hardwood floors, bay windows, and crown molding. It even had a sitting room. You had to love a room devoted solely to one body position.

"This place is great, I'm very interested," I told her.

"That's good, dear."

"So, how do I officially make an offer?"

"Well, before we go any further, I need to see how you live."

I looked at her in puzzlement. "I'm sorry?"

"I need to see how you keep your place," she answered. "You know, make sure you're not a slob or something."

"Uh, slob?" I stammered. "Well, I'm actually very neat, but to tell you the truth, I'm not sure what any of that has to do with anything. I mean, I don't want to *rent* your house, I want to buy it, so I don't see why-- -"

"I won't sell to someone who doesn't live like I do, so I need to see your place," she snapped.

"Uh, well, ma'am, I think it's going to be tough to show you my house."

"Why?" she demanded. Her tone was growing more agitated.

"Because it's in Los Angeles."

"Los Angeles!" she exclaimed. "Why are you in Los Angeles?"

"I'm in the entertainment industry, and---"

"Okay, that's enough," she interrupted. "I'm not dealing with show biz people."

"But I'm not a 'show biz' person, I'm from here. That's why I want to move back and---"

"Don't make me call the police," she said sternly.

About this time, I was sure glad I hadn't accepted her offer of tea. It was probably full of arsenic. Then once she'd finished poisoning me, she'd bake me into her meatloaf. *Neatly*, of course.

"Fine, ma'am, I didn't mean to upset you," I said as I headed towards the front door. As she silently held the door open for me, I suddenly stopped, and turned to her.

"You know something, ma'am? Though I am from Pittsburgh, I'm also in show business. That doesn't make me a bad person. There's a lot of good people who work in Hollywood."

Sophie looked at me for a moment, and her stern look softened. She reached out and touched my arm.

"Young man," she said, "Can you tell me something?"

"Certainly, Sophie. What is it you want to know?"

She leaned in close to me, and whispered, "Is Tom Cruise gay?"

After my harrowing experience with Ma Barker, I went back to the Friendship Residence to visit with Dad before I left. Turk came by to take me to the airport, and stopped in to visit with Dad for a few minutes. I really wanted to tell Dad that I'd be back next time for good, but I knew it would turn into an argument, which I definitely didn't want to have on my way out the door. Instead, we talked about the stuff guys and their dads talk about, like the latest road construction going on up the street, and the prospects for the Pirates having a winning season. Finally, Dad and I said our good-byes. I leaned in to shake his hand, and he suddenly grabbed me and hugged me. I was really surprised, but I hugged him back and gave him a kiss on the forehead.

"We'll see you later, Mr. Driscoll," said Turk.

"See you later, guys. Give me a call when you get back to LA, Big Ed," Dad said with a wave.

"Will do, Dad," I answered, and closed Dad's apartment door behind me.

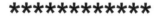

Back in LA, I'd just keyed into my front door when my phone rang. I dropped my luggage and grabbed it. "Welcome back!" came Ahmos' cheerful voice. "How was the flight from Pittsburgh?"

"Well, it was shorter than the drive from the airport, that's for sure. I won't miss the traffic out here."

"Hmm, well, funny you say that. Is there any way I could get you to experience just a little more LA traffic than you'd planned to?"

I sat down and sighed. "So, what's up?"

"Well," Ahmos continued, "I got an offer for a gig today."

"Good, you should do it," I replied.

"Well, they don't want me, it's for you...you know I respect whatever you want to do, but I was hoping you'd consider doing this one. Dick Clark is producing an awards show, and he's looking for someone to write it. "

"Listen Ahmos, I hear he's a great guy, but I'm completely focused on getting back to

Pittsburgh now. I mean, I just got held up in LA for eight extra months as it is, so I really have no interest in waiting any longer, which I'm sure you understand, right? Plus, you remember that I'm in escrow now. From what the real estate agent tells me, I don't think the new buyer will be willing to let me hang around this time."

There was a pause, then Ahmos lowered his voice. "Look, I really hate to even ask you, but it would really help me out if you did this gig. I'd like to develop my relationship with Dick and his people."

Nuts. There was no way I couldn't do a favor for one of my best friends, and a guy who'd been there for me, on stage and off, for my entire career. And I thought it was tough breaking *in* to show business. It seemed tougher to break *out* of it.

"Well, I'd probably do you more of a favor by letting you give them somebody *good* to do the show," I kidded. "But...listen, for me, I'd say 'no', but if it's for you, I say 'yes'."

"I appreciate it Ed, but I want to give you the full scoop before you say 'yes.' The project will take several weeks, but it shouldn't affect your escrow situation. However, it does mean that's several more weeks that you'll be delayed from your move back east."

"Oh, well, I've delayed this long, so what the hell," I said resignedly. "The lawyers indicated there's some possible glitch with the escrow, anyway."

"Yeah, I got cc'd on that email," Ahmos replied. "Escrow is a little more complicated than when that film company only had a deposit down, but it's actually something I can fix in about ten minutes, so don't make your decision based on that."

"No, Ahmos, I made my decision based on helping you. So yeah, if you can fix that escrow snafu, that'll be great, but I'm still sticking around for the gig. And I think it'll be cool to work with Dick Clark, maybe he'll give me his trademark salute!"

"Great, I appreciate it," Ahmos answered. "And hey, as my way of saying thanks, I got you booked to appear on Jim Rome's ESPN show this week. They tape practically down the street from you."

"Excellent, I'm a big fan of the show," I enthused. "That's a great 'thank you' gift."

"It was either that, or a Starbucks gift card," Ahmos joked.

"I already got one of those from my attorney as a Christmas gift last year," I replied. "That cappuccino cost me about ten thousand dollars."

★★★★★★★★★★★★

"Barry Bonds, the greatest player ever? What's your take, Ed?" I squinted through the studio lights at my inquisitor, Jim Rome. We were on the set of his popular ESPN show, "Jim Rome Is Burning." I waded into this one with relish.

"Well, he's the greatest ever, as long as it's not an important playoff game," I began. Though I knew damn well that Bonds probably *is* the best ever, I wasn't about to take up his mantle. I was still stinging from Bonds' inability to produce in three straight playoff appearances when he was an integral member of my beloved Pittsburgh Pirates. And the fact he'd been unable to make a decent throw in the last game of the NLCS against the Braves was the salt on the open-wound margarita. Of course, Barry's biggest offense to me was that he left the Pirates organization right after that game, and went on to greener free-agency pastures in California. It felt to me like he'd betrayed the city of Pittsburgh by leaving. Maybe it was just a reflection of my own guilt for essentially doing the same thing! At any rate, about the only real "weakness" one could point to about Bonds was his great play during the regular season, but continual struggles in the post-season. "You know how Reggie Jackson was 'Mr. October'?" I offered. "Well, Barry is 'Mr. September.'"

278

The other panelists laughed, though they disagreed. I plowed on.

"You know who he really is? He's Michigan J. Frog, that singing frog from the Warner Brothers cartoon. He can belt 'em out with the best of them, but when it's time to sing for the important folks, he goes back to 'ribbit-ribbit."

Jim got on me pretty good, as only he can, and finally I admitted: "Okay, fine. He might be the best player ever, but I'm the most bitter Pirates fan ever."

Jim smirked, then said, "Clearly."

After the taping, Ahmos and I went out to dinner, and I brooded about the appearance. I wondered if I'd gone a little too far in ridiculing Bonds. "I almost feel a little guilty," I told Ahmos.

"Listen, Bonds doesn't even care what his own teammates think about him, so why would he care about what some comedian he's never even heard of says?"

I looked at him, and feigned being hurt.
"Gosh, thanks a lot," I murmured.
"You know what I'm saying," Ahmos
answered.
Actually, I did, and it was a pretty funny
point, too. Besides, I had several friends in
the media who'd dealt with Bonds, and to a
person they described him as singularly
unpleasant. My Catholic guilt started to
fade, and I started thinking ahead to the job
I was to start the next morning. A job that
would finally be my last one in LA.

With my spirits slightly dragging, I
showed up at the offices of Dick Clark
Productions in the morning to begin work. I
was supposed to write the script for the
"Family Friendly TV" awards show, which I
considered re-titling the "Oxymoron"
awards show, considering how unfriendly
most of TV is for families.
I wasn't sure why, but I was having a
hard time getting my work energy up to its
usual level. I tried to shake the cobwebs

from my head and give myself a little Knute Rockne pep talk, a sort of "win one for the hipper." It's going to be a fun project, I told myself. I didn't really know the producer I was working with, Barry Adelman. But he seemed pleasant, and he had a goofy, twisted sense of humor like me. A bit ironic that we were in charge of the "family friendly" material.

Barry introduced me to Dick Clark, and it was fun to meet a guy who'd seemingly been around since the beginning of time, yet somehow looked younger than me. I believe his original promo photos were taken by Matthew Brady.

Dick said, *"Hello, Ed"* in that perfect, smooth, announcer voice of his, and I almost giggled out loud. I had met a lot of famous people, and it really didn't do much for me by this point, but meeting certain people that I grew up watching still gave me a happy jolt. For instance, I was really excited when I met Henry Winkler, whom everybody knows as "The Fonz." And now this was another of those "guy from the television of my youth standing right in front of me" moments. Cool stuff! I resisted the urge to make some bad "American Bandstand" joke.

"So, Ed," Dick continued. "What thoughts do you have about all this?"

"Well, actually, I've been thinking, "I'm glad I'm quitting the business." He and Barry laughed, not realizing that I was serious. Once again, those great side benefits of being a comedian, you can make all kinds of passive-aggressive, incredibly honest comments, and people think you're joking.

For the moment, though, I knew I owed it to Barry, and Dick Clark, and Ahmos, and myself for that matter, to "play hurt" as athletes say, to work hard and deliver, despite not feeling particularly well. With a reserve I was thankful to find, I threw myself into writing the script. In a matter of several days, I was quite pleased with what I had down on paper.

Barry and I got together on Sunday afternoon and went over everything we'd written, and cemented our plans to tape the show on Wednesday night. Barry was happy, Dick was happy, and hopefully, the network people would be happy. Then, I'd be...well, as long as everyone else was happy, that might be as close to happiness as I could hope for, at least for the time being.

Early Monday morning, about five o'clock, my phone rang. I sat up with a start, wondering who the hell that could be? Maybe Barry? But we had just been working all day, what could we possibly have forgotten to do? Bleary-eyed, I grabbed the phone. It was Melissa. "Eddie, come quick. Dad's dying."

I threw some clothes into an overnight bag and headed to LAX. I bought a ticket over the phone on the first flight I could get, which unfortunately wasn't until ten-thirty Pacific time that morning. Dad had collapsed at the Residence a few hours ago, and had been rushed to St. Clair hospital, the very hospital where Mom had undergone several cancer procedures. Keira and Melissa were at his side, and Caitlin and Robert were desperately trying to get there from New York. They were catching a flight in several hours as well, and would be there before me. I prayed to get there in time to say good-bye.

I was in a daze at the airport. I picked up my ticket, and headed into one of the longest security lines I'd ever seen. I called Ahmos to tell him what was going on, and asked him to call Barry, and Dick Clark, to let them know I had to leave, and wouldn't be at the taping this week. I was glad I'd turned in the script the day before, just so I wouldn't leave them hanging too badly. As I stood in line at security, my phone rang. It was Melissa, telling me Dad had passed away peacefully after receiving last rites. I shouted, "NO!" and dropped to my knees,

and people behind me in line merely went
around me and through the metal detectors
as I stood wobblily back up and composed
myself. Remarkably, or perhaps not, not one
person nearby acknowledged me or asked if
I was okay. Everyone in LA was wrapped up
in their own lives. It was hard to conceive of
nobody stopping to check on me if this had
occurred in a smaller town, say, Pittsburgh.

I went through security, and made my
way to the gate. No tears, no anger, no
sadness, just complete numbness. I sat at
the gate, and they announced a delay of at
least an hour with my flight. I dazedly
scanned the faces of people around me.
"My Dad just died, right now, and these
people have no idea," I ruminated over and
over, as I looked at everyone carrying on
with their lives. I wondered how many times
I'd sat across from somebody at an airline
gate, oblivious to the fact that they were
on the way home to the funeral of a loved
one. Who knew what was going on in
people's worlds, as they sat and read or

slept or chatted or simply stared. We spend a lot of time interacting with each other, yet most of the time we have no idea what's really going on in the next person's head. All around us, the cycle of life moves relentlessly forward, with no special regard for anyone, or anything.

Due to terrible weather, and a delay of over two hours before even taking off from LAX, I arrived in Pittsburgh late that evening. I went straight to Melissa's, where everyone had gathered to form one big, sad, exhausted group. Nobody spoke, we all just sat staring out the window at the driving August rain. Dad had passed away two days after what would have been Mom's eighty-first birthday.

As I called my home answering machine back in LA, I was surprised to discover a huge amount of voicemails expressing sympathy. I hadn't told anyone but Ahmos about Dad's death, but when he mentioned it to my agency, word seemed

286

to spread quickly. The biggest surprise wasn't really the number of calls, but rather who the calls were from. I knew my closest friends would be calling and showing up for the funeral if they were able to do so, but I didn't expect so many entertainment industry people to call my machine. Many of them I knew at only a very superficial level, and it was touching that they'd taken time to express heartfelt condolences. Donations flooded into the hospice in Dad's name from people I'd only worked with on one project, often for just a few days. The people at Dick Clark's company were incredible, and told Ahmos they intended to pay me for the entire "Family Awards" show, even though I'd be missing several of the most critical days, including the actual taping. My sense of cynicism for show business received quite a jolt as a result of all this unexpected outpouring of family values from an industry generally regarded as notoriously self-absorbed.

After leaving Melissa's place, I went back to Ann and Turk's house, and they were still up, waiting for me. Ann excitedly told me, "I have to show you something. Come here!" She led me upstairs to my usual guest room, and flipped on the lights. Nothing happened. I gave her a puzzled look.

"The light bulbs blew out again! Right after you called to tell me about your dad! Honest to God, he's here!"

Turk walked into the room, and Ann pointed at him. "What did I tell you guys?" she asked triumphantly. "I left the burned-out bulbs in their sockets, as proof!"

Turk said, "Honey, it's proof that lightbulbs are burned out, but beyond that...." his voice trailed off, and he looked at me.

"Well, if all that lightbulb stuff hadn't happened after Mom's death, I'd think nothing of this, but given that..."

"So you believe Van Praagh is right after all?" asked Ann hopefully.

288

"I'm not sure," I demurred. "I'd love to believe it, but you can never underestimate how poorly some companies make their products. Where did you buy these bulbs?" Ann gave an exasperated sigh.

"I'm sorry," I said. "I don't know the answer for sure, and if you believe this was my dad's doing, well, that's certainly okay by me."

The following morning, I found myself back at Beinhauers funeral home, talking to Scott. Dad had made all his arrangements when we'd been there regarding Mom, so it was pretty simple. I thanked Scott for how helpful he and his crew had been, and we decided on the same schedule we'd had for Mom: a private funeral, then a memorial service for everyone else the following week.

At Beinhauers the very next day, the day of Dad's funeral, I met Father Jim, who'd taken over as pastor just a month earlier for Father Richmond, who'd retired, and wasn't doing particularly well due to his diabetes. Father Jim was a young man with a round, kind face, and a gentle manner to match. He had been the one to give Dad his last rites, and Keira had told me that he had talked directly to Dad the entire time, as though Dad was conscious. Father Jim had introduced himself to our dying father, saying he was sorry to meet Dad under these circumstances, but that he'd heard so many good things about him from all the parishioners at St. John's.

We all had our private time with Dad laying in his casket. He looked so peaceful, but I was so sorry I hadn't gotten there in time to say "good-bye." But then, maybe I had, because I'd been able to say good-bye after we'd been to the baseball game. Thank God I hadn't delayed that trip into Pittsburgh to work on Troy Miller's show. It suddenly occurred to me that maybe Dad had hugged me on purpose the last time I'd seen him, as though he'd known he was leaving soon. My eyes welled up at the memory of that moment, and I hugged him one last time.

Father Jim led a beautiful ceremony, speaking at length about the many testimonials regarding Dad he'd received from so many parishioners. He told us that when he'd announced Dad's death at morning mass, there'd been an audible gasp from the congregation. Father's words were positive and upbeat, and he said he pictured God welcoming Dad into heaven with the words, "Well done, Edward."

We all stayed in Pittsburgh, since Dad's memorial mass was being held in just a few days. The whole thing felt surreal, even more so than when Mom had passed. At least back then, we still had Dad to spend time with and take care of, and it infused all our lives with a sense of purpose. But now, there were no parents. I was angry with myself for not moving back to Pittsburgh soon enough. Now, I'd become an orphan at age forty, all in the span of nine months. Even though I was an adult, I felt lost, confused. Basically, in nine months, I'd become a baby again. What was it with babies and the nine months thing?

I once again found myself at the podium at St. John's church, once again having to speak in a situation I'd somehow hoped I'd never have to face. I didn't even bother to try writing anything down in advance this time, having learned from Mom's mass that it's best to just say whatever comes to mind. Hopefully, the spirit of my parents would be my muse.

I looked out at the group of mourners, which included many people from out of town who had been unable to attend Mom's mass in the late fall. I smiled at the large contingent representing the Friendship Residence: the owners, plus a lot of the staff and many residents, including a woman named Twyla, who was now using Dad's wheelchair. We knew Dad would want her to have it, since hers was an old rickety model. When I'd approached her with the

292

offer of Dad's chair, she'd started to cry, and said she'd be truly honored.

"We have to stop meeting like this, people," I began, to some nervous laughter, mostly my own. "I have to tell you folks that, knowing my dad as you did, and how he never wanted any fuss over him, we had to pressure him to have a memorial mass. I mean, we didn't pressure him to pass away, but when he was planning his estate, he said he didn't want any sort of public memorial. I told him that his friends would want to say good-bye. He said, 'Hey, at my age, people are always telling me good-bye.'" The church filled with warm laughter, and I continued the story.

"So, I finally said, come on, Dad, it's important for us to honor you. And he said, 'I don't want you guys to have to get up there and try to talk about me, and end up crying, and everybody just feels worse.' And I told him, 'Gee, Dad, you're sure making it a lot easier to not cry when we have to get up there.'" More laughter.

I spoke of my regret at not having asked Dad to move a chess piece like I'd asked of Mom, and said, "Dad, I know you're listening now, so please make a move if you can." I started to choke up, and said, "Oops, there you go, Dad, I almost did start crying!"

As our friends and family chuckled sympathetically, I drew a deep breath and continued. "Let me just finish by thanking you all for sharing in this celebration of the life of the two finest people I've ever known, my parents. Anything good I've ever done on this earth, anything helpful or kind or giving in any way, comes from their influence, and I know my sisters and I will always be thankful to them."

As I was making my way to my car after mass, I heard a voice behind me. "More humor, and more sorrow. It's been quite a year for you, Ed." I turned around to see Mrs. Angie, Mom's close friend, standing there, leaning on a cane.

"Well, I guess humor and sorrow are pretty much inseparable," I said.

"Yes, just like your parents were inseparable. And now they're together again."

I smiled at her, then pointed to her cane. "You weren't using that last time I saw you," I said, then immediately realized how inappropriate it was for me to blurt that out. Certainly she was aware of her cane, I don't know why I felt compelled to make reference to it.

"Yes, well, I hurt my ankle a few months ago. I think my rugby career might be over."

Her remark caught me by surprise, and I laughed that great kind of laugh that only comes when you least expect to be laughing.

She looked down at her cane and shook her head. "The body isn't meant to last, but the sense of humor is. Because it's part of the soul."

We chatted for a few more minutes, I thanked her for coming, and wished her the best on her comeback attempt in professional sports.

I drove back to Melissa's place, and many people came and brought food, much as they'd done that day we'd moved Mom and Dad out of the Tyris house. It was hard to believe that day had been only about a year ago. With all that had happened, it seemed like decades.

Strangely, the atmosphere this time was more festive than it had been on moving day. It certainly wasn't that people were glad my parents had died, but I guess back when they'd moved out of the neighborhood, it felt to people like they were truly losing my folks, while this gathering ironically seemed more like a pure celebration of Mom and Dad's lives. Just as at Dad's funeral, and at his memorial mass, everyone spoke of both Dad *and* Mom, because, as Father Jim pointed out, "You can't talk about one without talking about the other. That's how close they were to each other, and their community."

After the guests had helped clean up and gone on their way, our family sat down in Melissa's living room and collectively exhaled. We started talking about the estate, and the meeting we had with the lawyer the following day. I had been chosen as the executor, and everyone was comfortable with that decision. Everyone except me, that is. Oh, I was flattered and all, and was certainly more than willing to honor my parents' last request. But I knew it would be an unpleasant task. I did my best not to show my feelings, however, because I knew I had to be an example for my sisters to draw strength from. I kidded about cutting everyone out of the will, and spending it all on PlayStation games for me and my nephews. Ronan was disappointed to find out I was kidding.

As for Mom and Dad's belongings, they'd stipulated that we decide amongst

297

ourselves what to keep and what to give away. Keira observed, "Really, none of the things in this world belong to anybody. We're merely caretakers, passing them on from one generation to the next." I raised an eyebrow, looked at her and asked, "Keira, have you been writing dialogue for Yoda?"

We donated the bulk of the furniture to "Emmaus House," a home for mentally challenged adults. The facility was founded by friends of our parents, Lorraine and Ken Wagner. They had a child with a disability, and had quit their jobs to dedicate themselves to the formation and upkeep of Emmaus House. Ever since their daughter's birth, their lives were about making things better not only for their own offspring, but for anyone else finding themselves in the same situation. Talk about meaningful lives. Almost every person in the world knows the names "Paris Hilton," or "Ryan Seacrest," yet almost nobody has ever heard of

"Lorraine and Ken Wagner." How sick is that?

The same day Dad died, hockey coach Herb Brooks had also died, in an automobile accident in Minnesota. As I'd listened to the platitudes given Brooks, by all his former players and people whose lives he'd touched, I remembered thinking, "He must have been a good man, it's nice that so many people get to hear of his good works in this life." But I also felt sad that not nearly as many people were talking about my dad, at least not on radio and television, and I regretted there wasn't some forum for more people to know just what a decent man Dad had been. But then, people who aren't "famous" are dying every day, and we usually are unaware of it unless we knew them, or knew somebody who knew them. Not that it matters anyway, I guess. As Chester said, at the end of the game, all the pieces go back in the same box.

The next morning, I spoke at Carl Kurlander's "Creative Writing" class at the University of Pittsburgh. The students seemed quite interested in my adventures in Hollywood, and I particularly enjoyed the question-and-answer period. I pointed at Carl and told the class, "Wow, doesn't it feel good to ask the questions, rather than have to answer his?"

There were a lot of interesting queries, ranging from, "What's the worst thing you've ever written? (A: "I like to think it's yet to come.") to "Can you get me a job?" (A: "No.")

One question in particular stopped me in my tracks: "What among your work so far do you feel is the most meaningful?" I blinked and looked at the earnest face of the young woman who'd asked it, just to make sure she'd actually said it, and it hadn't just come from inside my own head. "Um, well, I guess 'meaningful' is a relative term," I began, and the class laughed, though I wasn't really trying to be funny. I muttered something about us all having to find our own meaning, then quickly asked for another question. I felt like a presidential press spokesman dodging a question that was embarrassing to the administration.

After the class, some of the students approached Carl and I, and we chatted with them informally for a bit. Some of the kids had questions about midterms and other academic matters, and it was interesting to observe Carl in his "professor" mode, especially when he admonished some of the kids he'd deemed as slackers to get their "asses in gear."

"Wow, the teachers didn't talk like that to the kids on 'Saved By The Bell,'" I kidded him.

"Well, maybe if they had, the show would still be running," Carl answered.

After the last student had wandered off, Carl and I went to the coffee shop in the student union. We chatted about mutual friends in California, and he told me of a program he was starting called

"Pittsburghers in Hollywood," that would involve people such as myself speaking to his class on a regular, rotating basis. In addition, it would be a way to network, and get together with other Pittsburghers in Los Angeles from time to time. For a city that was small by many standards, Pittsburgh had a surprising number of players in Hollywood, including Dennis Miller, Rob Marshall (Director of "Chicago"), George Benson, Michael Keaton, and others.

"That's a great concept, Carl. You know, you seem really happy with being a professor, and everything you're doing here."

"I really am, Ed."

We sat in silence for a moment, then Carl asked, "So, that young woman really threw you with that 'meaningful work' question, huh?"

"Um, why would you say that?"

"It just seemed like the only time all day you were uncomfortable."

302

"I guess so," I admitted. "With all that's happened, Carl, it's hard to say what my life is really about. I mean, everything was good and satisfying for awhile. But then my engagement broke up, then other relationships didn't work out, then I started questioning what I do for a living, then I thought maybe I'll move back to Pittsburgh for a more 'normal' life and to be around my aging parents. Before I could do that, my mom died, then I thought, okay, that does it, I'll move back to Pittsburgh to care for my dad, maybe *that's* what I'm meant to do on this earth. And then, Dad dies, too. It's hard not to feel a bit at sea right about now. But I still think I need to come back to Pittsburgh, even without my folks, because I still have my sister here, and my nephews. Plus, my LA house is in escrow now anyway, and it wouldn't be easy to get out of that as opposed to when it was just a deposit down on the house, and..."

My voice trailed off as I realized I was rambling, and Carl smiled sympathetically.

"Listen, lots of people go through questions of what they're doing, where they should live, all the stuff you're talking about. These issues are on any thinking person's mind, from adults to teens. Hell, we dealt with these questions, at least, in a certain way, back on 'Saved by The Bell.'"

"Hmm," I mused. "So the question really is, what would Screech do?"

Carl laughed. "Yeah, I guess you could put it that way."

"Carl, I read somewhere that the actor who played Screech, what's his name?"

"Dustin Diamond."

"Yeah, I read that he's a big chess enthusiast. Is that true?"

"Of course," said Carl. "But what did you expect? Screech was a total geek."

★★★★★★★★★★★

I couldn't clear my head. I feared I was lost. Nothing made any sense, plus I was clearly running out of time.

Finally, I sighed, and used my mouse to drop my pawn to rook three. Immediately, Chessmaster 5000 pounced on this slight inaccuracy by pushing its king onto my fourth rank, and I realized the position was lost. Shit! That's the thing about dealing with computers. They don't make even minor mistakes, let alone the type of major blunders human beings so often commit. It's not like the computer was mourning the loss of its parents. *"Dear Mr. PowerMac, we're sorry to inform you that Mr. and Mrs. Macintosh were found frozen in an office worker's cubicle. Efforts to re-boot them were unsuccessful."* Of course, computers didn't get to experience the upside of life, either. The joy of music, or laughter, or sex. Come to think of it, neither did I. At least, not lately.

"This game is a microcosm of my life," I said aloud even though I was alone, much as soap actors do when they're trying to re-cap the plot for infrequent viewers. Instead of hitting the "resign" button, I childishly popped the CD-ROM out of my disc drive, and Frisbeed it across my office.

Enough isolating. It was time for some human contact. Of course, by "contact" I didn't mean actually interacting with another human, but rather, checking my email.

Since I'd been back in LA, I'd become somewhat of a recluse, a la Howard Hughes near the end, minus the jars of urine. So many people had been calling to see how I was, which of course I appreciated. But I was finding it extremely difficult to pick up that nine-hundred-pound phone receiver. Thank God for my answering machine. I felt guilty every time I walked past and saw another phone message that I had no heart to return, at least not yet.

I'd wanted to lose myself in some chess, but going to the chess club only reminded me of Chester, which in turn reminded me of my parents, which in turn reminded me of the fragility of our lives, which in turn reminded me that there didn't seem to be a lot of meaning to anything in mine right now. Talk about seeing many moves ahead! So, I'd decided to take on my electronic opponent, a decision I regretted the second I made that stupid pawn move.

Switching gears, I scanned the subject lines of my email. I began deleting the myriad of messages offering Viagra, Prozac, and sometimes *both!* I guess that's for those who are fucking depressed.

One email was an advertisement reading "It's not too late to order flowers for you mother!!" I hit reply and typed, "Actually, it is. Please delete me from your marketing list." Bastards. I moved on. I had a message from Rita, my ex-fiancée, expressing her sorrow over my parents' passing. For whatever reason, instead of comforting me, her email only made me feel worse. I knew that wasn't her intent, but unfortunately, it was the result.

A few hours later, I flipped on the television to watch SportsCenter, and discovered that Barry Bonds' father, Hall of Famer Bobby Bonds, had passed away after a long bout with cancer. I suddenly felt sick about what I'd said on Jim Rome's show. Actually, everything I'd said was pretty true, but for the first time, I saw Bonds as a fellow human, a grieving son, and felt empathy with him. Whether he'd want me to or not was irrelevant.

I turned the TV back off. Man, there was no getting away from this death stuff, not even a brief respite. As Executor of the estate, all of Mom and Dad's mail was forwarded to me, which meant every day I received letters, bills, checks, magazines, and junk mail, all with my parents' names on them. It was like getting a telegram every day: *In case you forgot, your parents are dead. Stop.*

Just what exactly did that even mean, anyway, "dead?" I couldn't even begin to really comprehend it. I walked into my living room and spoke to the ceiling. "Dad! Mom! Are you there? Is anybody there?" It was like a posthumous version of that cell phone commercial. *"Can you hear me now?"*

Could they hear me? Could they see me? If so, how exactly were they viewing me? Were they actually in the room with me? Or were they watching on a giant, theatre-like screen? Or maybe little TV monitors? Did they watch me all the time, or were there other shows on up there, too? MASH re-runs, maybe? Man, I'll bet that's some sweet residuals for those writers.

Every day since their funerals, I'd asked for more signs from my parents. Not just regarding the chess pieces, but signs like they may have sent me before, such as the lightbulbs flickering out. But my requests had gone unanswered. I didn't blame my folks, maybe it just wasn't possible to make specific requests. This was a bit hard to accept at times, I guess because we've all been spoiled by the incredible technologies available on this earth. I mean, it sure seemed that if I could watch movies on my cell phone, then certainly I should be able to get my folks to flick lights on a more regular basis. But I guess the only thing harder to believe in than miracles was the idea of miracles on demand, like some sort of pay-per-view event you can order up with your remote control.

I pulled up a chair in front of my chessboard, and grabbed a book off the shelf by one of my favorite chess authors, Jeremy Silman. I started flipping through it, trying to decide on a game to analyze, when a particular paragraph caught my eye:

> In chess, a plan is really just making positive use of the existing characteristics of a position. You have to do what the position is telling you to do. You don't do what you want to do, you do what the position requires. There is often a big difference between these two things.

Where had I seen this before? This was a
new book, how could I have read this part
already? Then, a chill went up my spine as I
thought back to Dad, sitting in his hospital
bed telling me that *"...life is always pointing
each of us in the right direction, telling us
what to do. It may not even be what you
want to do, but it's what circumstances
dictate that you SHOULD do. We're the
ones who choose to either do what it's
showing us, or to resist it and be unhappy."*
Slightly unnerved, I closed the book, and
decided to go to bed early.

****

"Well, here we go again, Ed." Billy
Crystal's voice rang out from my answering
machine. "Looking forward to working
together again."
Billy had just been announced as the host
of the Academy Awards for 2004, and he
was expecting me to be with him as a writer
on the telecast. I was flattered as always,
and my favorite times in show business had

311

been the projects I'd done with him in the past, especially the Oscars. Clearly this would be yet another delay from moving to Pittsburgh, but there was no way I'd pass up another opportunity to work with one of my very favorite people.

I sat down at my computer and started writing jokes for possible use by Billy. As the afternoon wore on, I scanned the Hollywood trade papers and tapped on the keyboard. Eventually, I took a look at what I had written so far:

Welcome to the Oscars, where we celebrate the greatest medium in the world, the movies, by putting on a television show.

There was a lot of nakedness in the movies this year, wasn't there? I haven't seen that much flesh since...well, since the red carpet entrance a few minutes ago.

I loved "Master and Commander." Russell Crowe fought five guys at once. And that was at the wrap party.

I loved "House of Sand and Fog." Hey, who isn't rooting for Shohreh Aghdashloo to win? Well, actually, maybe one person: the engraver.

You know what the scariest thing about "Kill Bill Volume One" is? The words, "Volume One."

"Lord Of The Rings" is three hours and eighteen minutes. I normally don't watch anything that long unless it involves bats and gloves.

The Academy is very happy with doing the Oscars earlier this year, so I'm pleased to announce that next year's Oscars will be held...later tonight. People always ask, 'What's Oscar's last name?' Obviously, it's "Goes-to."

It's been a great year for the movies. And to those critics who say Hollywood has lost its creativity, I say... just check out the studios' accounting procedures.

A lot of people get up here and don't know how to express their gratitude. Sometimes, that's because they've never done it before.

Not a bad start, I thought as I sat back in my chair. Suddenly, the doorbell rang. My instinct was to ignore it, but I was expecting some shipments, so I knew I had to go to the door. Damn, forget about the phone, I needed a door-answering machine.

Sure enough, it was UPS, with five large boxes. Really *high-quality* boxes I mused, as I ran my hand over their edges admiringly, drawing an odd look from the UPS driver. I snapped out of my state of container awe and signed for the delivery, then dragged the boxes into the kitchen to begin the excavation process.

The first thing out of the first box turned out to be Dad's cane. I smiled at the thought of how long it took for him to start actually using it. The next few items were from Mom's collection of Belleek china. She'd purchased several pieces when she and Dad had visited Ireland, and though I tried to encourage my sisters to take them all, they insisted I have several pieces as well. As I looked at it, I was glad they had insisted. The box also contained several other sculptures from Mom's collection, including a beautiful rendition of the Holy Family, and several plates of Franciscan china decorated with autumn leaves. I smiled at the fact that even after her death, Mom was still sending me fall leaves. As I stared at the china, I realized where I'd seen it before. It's featured prominently in the movie "The Sixth Sense." An interesting coincidence. *I see dead people's dinner plates.*

I tried to get back to working on Oscar material, but I couldn't get my parents out of my mind. I finally gave up the notion of getting anything else written, and shut down my computer. As I sat staring at the now black screen, I suddenly heard whoosh!

"What in the world?" I thought as I got up to investigate. It sounded like someone lighting a stove or something. I walked into my kitchen, but nothing was awry. Suddenly, out of the corner of my eye, I saw a fire blazing in the living room. Fortunately, it was in the fireplace, so there was no need for alarm. The noise I'd heard was gas igniting the fire, which happens when someone presses the remote control. However, I hadn't pressed anything. Furthermore, the fireplace had been broken for several months. I'd been meaning to have it repaired, but hadn't gotten around to it. Yet here I stood, staring at a blazing fire.

I guess it's working again, I thought. But I wonder how it got triggered? Must have been some sort of misfire with the lighting mechanism, or something. After all, what else could it be, right? I looked on the mantle above the fireplace at a picture of me and Dad, taken at the ballgame in Pittsburgh, less than a week before his death.

"Is that you, Dad?" I said out loud. "Are you trying to talk to me? How am I supposed to know what's going on?" I exclaimed in exasperation. I turned to the picture next to it, one of me and Mom in front of the Television Academy. "Mom, why can't you and Dad just call me or something..."

At that precise moment, the phone rang. After briefly pausing to change my underwear, I picked up the receiver. It was my friend Jon Macks. "Hey, Ed, did I catch you at a bad time?"

"Actually, yes. I'm awake. What's up, Jon?"

"Well, I just wanted to let you know my book's been published, and I've sent you a copy."

"Hey, congrats. I assume you're calling because you want a check?" I needled.

"No checks, just cash," Jon continued. "Listen, there was a bit of a snafu, though. You're quoted quite extensively throughout the book."

"Is that the snafu?"

"No, it's just that you're referred to as "Eddie" Driscoll all through the book. I'm not sure how it happened, but it's already gone to print."

Oh, man. I knew I was in for an ordeal with the Writers Guild, Screen Actors Guild, and hell, probably the Lollipop Guild, because my professional name is always supposed to be "Ed" Driscoll, so that "Eddie" Driscoll and I are differentiated. Ugh.

"Hey, Jon, no problem."

"I'm sorry, Ed, I know it will be a bit of a hassle for you. I really don't know why they wrote "Eddie." I'd written your name as "Ed." Nobody calls you Eddie, right?"

"Exactly. Well, except for my sisters, and my mom...." I stopped cold. Was this a sign from Mom? Or was I just looking for *anything* that could be interpreted as a sign? I remembered that Jon had called me "Eddie" during that phone call we'd had right after Mom's death. I wasn't sure what to make of it.

"Hey, Jon, congrats on the book, and don't worry about the "Ed/Eddie" thing. I look forward to reading it."

I hung up the phone, and looked at Dad and Mom's picture again. After a moment of thought, I said aloud, "Is that you guys sending me a message? Or just some incompetent proof-reader?" Unfortunately, there was no reply, at least, not one that I could hear.

****

    I pulled into the crowded parking lot of the Avalon Theatre, a landmark building in Los Angeles. I remembered having taped a show for NBC at that very venue a few years before, when it had been known as "The Hollywood Palace," a name it held for decades. It had recently changed its moniker. Nothing stays the same in Hollywood.

    Because it was only a few weeks before Christmas, there was a bit of a chill in the air, at least, what passes for a chill in LA. It was probably sixty degrees. Christmas in LA is something that never seemed quite right to me. Seeing Santa in shorts made him look like some sort of crazed flasher or something. I was always glad to be back in Pittsburgh over the holidays, though it certainly wouldn't be the same this year. In fact, it would not be the same ever, in any year.

I met up with my friend Mike in front of the theater, and we excitedly picked up our tickets at the will-call window. Our favorite band, REM, was playing a semi-private concert for its fan club and its record label, Warner Brothers, and we'd snagged some tickets through a connection.

I'd been to many REM shows over the years, catching every tour since 1987, and always found the occasion to be a nearly spiritual experience. There was nothing quite like the healing power of music, and it seemed like REM was always there for me through the good times and the bad. Unbeknownst to them, they were basically providing the soundtrack for my life.

Mike and I raced inside the minute the doors flung open. There were no seats, just a giant ballroom in front of the stage. As we rushed to get the best standing spots, I suddenly imagined us turning up on the news as victims in the latest rock 'n roll trampling incident. Fortunately, the crowd was remarkably polite, owing I'm certain in no small part to the fact that the band members, as well as a large contingent of its fans, were now in their forties.

At nine sharp, Michael Stipe and company hit the stage, and the crowd erupted. For what seemed like the first time in months, I felt energized, alive, in touch with all my senses. Especially when the guy in front of me dropped his beer on my foot.

Early on, the band played one of their older, more obscure songs, "Sweetness Follows." Though I had been to many of their concerts over the years, I'd never heard them perform it live. Suddenly, the words came rushing through me:

Readying to bury your father and your mother,
what did you think when you lost another?

My God, I'd forgotten about that line, or maybe, I had just never paid much attention to it. The song continued, and I could swear that Stipe was looking right at me as he sang:

It's these little things, they can pull you under.
Live your life filled with joy and thunder.
Yeah, yeah we were altogether,
lost in our little lives.
Oh, oh, but sweetness follows.
Oh, oh, but sweetness follows.

I arrived back home late that night, exhausted but happy following such a great evening of music, and noticed that I had one message on my answering machine. It was from my real estate agent. Apparently, the people who'd bid on my LA house had some sort of financial complication, and they'd fallen out of escrow.

322

"I'll pick you up right outside US Air baggage claim, Uncle Ed."

"Thanks, Seamus. I'll see you in a minute." I flipped my cell phone closed and headed out the door. It was Christmas eve morning, and I'd just flown the redeye from LA to Pittsburgh. Surprisingly, my baggage had arrived on the same flight as me.

A blast of cold air hit me as I walked outside, and right on time, Seamus pulled up to the curb. It was so strange to see him driving. He'd just earned his license, and had insisted that he pick me up that morning. I smiled at the memory of when I'd first acquired my license. I'd wanted to drive everywhere, run every possible errand that would involve me driving Dad's car. My sisters were more than happy to let Seamus pick me up, after all, they weren't exactly clamoring for the privilege of driving to the airport during the holiday rush.

Seamus swung the New Yorker into the passenger loading zone. It was Dad's car, which he'd promised Seamus he could have when he turned sixteen. Dad had known for awhile that he himself couldn't drive anymore, but he kept the car around for his grandson. I was just sorry he wasn't there to see Seamus driving it now.

I hopped into the passenger seat, and immediately turned down the radio, which of course was blasting at top volume. Wow, more proof that I was getting older. Twenty years earlier, the first thing I'd have done would've been to turn the music *up*.

With his own money he'd saved from his part-time job, Seamus had installed a new sound system, complete with CD player.

"Wow, imagine what Grandpa would say to hear this baby," I said.

Seamus grinned, and said, "He'd probably say, 'Turn that down!'

"And he'd be right!" I exclaimed, and we both laughed.

As we rode along, I couldn't help but have a bit of envy regarding Seamus, and all the excitement that was still ahead of him.

324

Man, to be sixteen, with a license, and just beginning to date, and nothing to do but go to school and have fun with your friends! What a great, anxiety-free life! If only I could do it again, if only I was back where Seamus was, if only... I caught myself, and chuckled. Yeah, "if only" the whole "anxiety-free" thing was actually real! I seemed to be suffering from the adult version of "the grass is always greener" syndrome. Though I had certainly enjoyed my teenage years, they were far from "anxiety-free." Sure, the issues back then may not have been as weighty as they were now in adulthood, such as paying bills, etc. But in reality, I was no less stressed as a teen than I was now. If my teen concerns were trivial by adult standards, they certainly didn't feel that way to me at the time. The fact is, there really is no "perfect age." Each stage of life comes with two sides, advantages and disadvantages. I guess it mostly depends on which side one chooses to live.

We arrived at Melissa's place right at the same time Caitlin and Robert came in from Saratoga. Keira had come in from Cleveland the day before, so now, our whole family was together, or at least, what was left of our family.

I checked out Melissa's Christmas tree, and saw all the bulbs with our names on them hanging from the branches. I had a sad memory flashback, recalling how special it had been when my dad had made a bulb for Rita, when we thought she was joining our family.

As I scanned up to the top of the tree, I burst out laughing.

When I was in first grade, our class had made "angel" decorations out of paper mache. The head was the size of a tennis ball, and was complete with yarn for the hair, eyes, and mouth. For some reason, I'd made my angel's mouth forming a giant, red "O", and when I brought it home, Keira had observed, "He looks like Mr. Bill!" (from Saturday Night Live.) He certainly did, and every year from then on, Mom had placed "Mr. Bill" on top of our tree. Now, here he was again, perched in his customary spot.

The next morning, Christmas day, I opened the blinds of Turk's guestroom to see snowflakes gently dropping from the sky. It was just the right amount, enough to have a white Christmas, yet not so much that you'd end up skidding off the road and wrapping the car around somebody's front-yard nativity set. Seamus picked me up and we drove to St. John's to meet the rest of the family at Mass.

When we got to the church and settled into our pew, my sisters started tearing up. I felt sad, but rather numb. How could this be Christmas without Mom and Dad? I was keeping it together until the opening hymn,
"Oh Come, All Ye Faithful." I'd purposely been avoiding listening to any Christmas music, because it made me too sad under the present circumstances. But there was

327

no avoiding it in church, and as I tried to sing, I had to stop, and I bowed my head, hoping nobody would notice the hot tears that suddenly were streaming down my face.

Father Jim presided over the mass, and as he'd done at Dad's service, he gave a great homily, welcoming everyone, regardless of whether they attended every week, or once a month, or once a year, or didn't really even believe in all we were celebrating that day. His kind-hearted inclusiveness made me realize just what the Catholic church could, and should, be about. They certainly needed more clergy like him.

After Mass, we drove out to the mausoleum to visit Mom and Dad. Melissa had decorated their graves with little ceramic snowmen, each one marked with one of our names. We talked about how much Mom would love the decorations, and figured Dad would probably say, "You can decorate your Mother's area, but you don't need to put anything on my spot."

So this is where we celebrated Christmas as a family. We knew Mom and Dad would be happy we were all together, even under this state of affairs. As we stood solemnly, Seamus and Ronan suddenly started wrestling each other. "Hey, guys, knock it off," Melissa said, but she was grinning. We all knew that Mom and Dad would appreciate the fact that their grandchildren were acting just as silly as they did when their grandparents were alive.

We went back to Melissa's place and ate brunch, Melissa preparing all the foods Mom used to make on Christmas, including homemade donuts. It was a surprisingly happy time, although, I guess I shouldn't have been so surprised. The human spirit has a way of enduring, and there was a lot of laughter as we invoked our parents' names repeatedly, speculating on what comments they'd make about various gifts.

Whenever my parents' faces flashed in my mind, I always saw them smiling and laughing, usually at some goofy thing I'd done or said.

★★★★★★★★★★★★

Late in the afternoon, I borrowed "Seamus's car," and drove to the Friendship Residence. As I guided the Chrysler through the front gates, I felt a knot in my stomach. I looked up at the windows of what had been Mom and Dad's place, right there on the first floor. Mom used to sit by the window when she was expecting me, and when I'd arrive she'd wave and buzz me in. The blinds were partially open, and I noticed a different decoration on the windowsill than had been there before. I guess there were new tenants in there now.

I drew a deep breath, and walked in the front door. I immediately ran into Twyla, the woman using Dad's wheelchair.

"Merry Christmas, Twyla. How are you?"

"Oh, Ed junior, Merry Christmas to you, dear. What are you doing here?"

"I came to see my friend Twyla," I said, and she smiled.

We visited for quite awhile, and she caught me up on the latest "gossip" involving the various residents. It's amazing, no matter how old one gets, it's always fun discussing the latest hearsay, or hard-of-hearsay, in this case.

I got to say hello to a lot of the people who were friends with my folks, and I was more than a little relieved to find out nobody had died since I'd last been there. Though of course death was inevitable, it was nice to have a break from it, if for only a little while. The thought ran through my head that of course, it could be *me* who passes away before any of these people do. Such is the unpredictability of our existence. But it's just the way things are, I reflected, and the more I accept it, the better I seem to deal with it.

I visited with several members of the staff, including chef Deke. Their laughter made me feel better than I had in months.

Eventually I made my way out to the car. I looked up at the window of Mom and Dad's old place, and the blinds were still half-open. I was sort of hoping I'd see them at the window, waving to me. I didn't see anyone, but I waved anyway, just in case.

Just as I got back to Turk's place, my cell phone rang.

"Hey, sorry to bother you," Ahmos' voice crackled through the earpiece.

"Since when are you sorry about bothering me?" I needled.

"Good point. Listen, I have an offer I want to run past you. Well, actually, I don't want to, because it's lousy, but until you officially leave LA, it's still my job to bring you whatever comes across my desk."

"What is it?" I asked.

"It's for a fledgling movie company. They're looking for some script help, or should I say, a *lot* of script help, on a romantic comedy. Honestly, their situation is pretty chaotic, and you'd basically be thrown immediately into the fire. It's an extremely tight deadline, they don't have much money, and you'd have to do a significant amount of traveling once they start filming."

"Wow, Ahmos, you sure know how to sell it."

"Sadly, that's about as good as I can sell it, the project's a mess. So, I'll tell them you'll pass."

"No, I'll take it."

"You'll take what?"

"The gig! Let's make a deal with them."

"Uh, well...you're joking, right?"

"No, I'm not."

"You'd have to stay in LA for awhile. It would definitely screw up your moving schedule."

"That's okay, I live in LA."

"Yeah, at the moment, but---"

"For the foreseeable future. I'm not moving back to Pittsburgh."

"Are you okay, Ed?"

"Yes, I'm more than okay. What, do you *want* me to move?"

"No, of course not, but...I mean, I'm really glad, but...why this gig?"

"Because it's what I do," I answered firmly. "The world needs laughter, right?"

Ahmos went silent for a moment. "Are you drinking again?"

"No!" I exclaimed. "Listen, did you ever see the movie "Stardust Memories?"

"By Woody Allen, sure."

"Well, then maybe you remember the scene where Woody meets the space aliens, and he says, 'Shouldn't I stop making movies and do something that counts? Like helping blind people, or becoming a missionary or something?,' and the alien says, "Hey, you're a comedian. You want to do mankind a real service? Write funnier jokes!'"

Ahmos laughed. "Yeah. So what about it?"

"Well, let's just say I'm coming back to LA to write funnier jokes."

"That's great, Ed. As long as this is truly what you want."

"It is. So, I guess this goes down as one of the shortest show business retirements in history, huh?"

"Not really. The truth is, you never really left the business in the first place."

****

I couldn't believe how the days flew by, and before I knew it, I was packing my things for the flight back to LA. Turk stuck his head into the guest bedroom as I crammed a bunch of the gifts I'd received into my garment bag.

"Need any help, sir?" he asked, in the mock tones of a bellhop.

"Yep, but unless you're a shrink, I don't think you can give it to me."

We sat down and talked about the holidays. Turk was exhausted from running around for the last week, to his parents' house, to Ann's parents' house, to the store, etc.

"You have no idea how good you have it," I said.

Turk replied, "Oh, but I do. Believe me." He paused a moment. "You know, I miss your folks too, Ed."

I knew he meant it. Turk had been great about looking in on them from time to time over the last few years, which had given me a lot of peace of mind. I thanked him for all he'd done, and he said it was his pleasure.

"So, Ed, are you gonna start doing your show again?" he asked.

"Yeah, man. I am."

Turk breathed a sigh of relief. "Good. I was getting the idea that you were fed up with things out there."

"Oh, don't think that I'm not, but...it's what I do, you know?"

Turk nodded. "Well, it's good you seem to be sure of yourself again." The room was silent for a moment, then Turk looked me in the eyes.

"Ed, do you think you'd ever move back here?"

I informed him that just yesterday, I'd purchased a grave plot in the mausoleum, right near my parents. I sure didn't want to use it for many years, but thought it would be nice when that time came. My sisters were planning on using some of their inheritance to do the same thing. Nine months previously, I'd have been way too creeped out to actually make arrangements like that, but now, it didn't bother me in the least. Dealing with life, and death, just didn't seem as scary anymore.

"So, to answer your question, Turk, yeah, I will move back to Pittsburgh...eventually, and for good. But for now, I've got to do what the position requires."

CHAPTER SEVEN

Late January 2004. I was back in LA. And as annoying and shallow as this town, and this business, can be at times, I no longer had any doubts about it being my destiny. I sat watching tapes of my show from six months earlier, preparing to perform "Mismatch Maker" again. I scribbled furiously in a notebook, recording ideas for improving the jokes.

The phone rang, and I answered to hear Melissa's voice, sounding distressed. "What's wrong, Mel?"

"I don't know, Eddie. I'm just feeling like Mom and Dad have forgotten about me."

"What do you mean?"

"Well, they seem to give you all kinds of signs, I swear they're always talking to you. But I've been asking them to give me a sign, let me know they're there, but nothing happens with me."

"I'm sure that's not the case, Mel. I have no doubt they are contacting you, but you're just not picking up on it. Believe me, even when it's right there in front of you, it's not always easy to see."

We spoke for a long time, and I told her to just try to keep her senses aware, and that I was sure she'd hear from our parents. As I hung up, I felt very sad for Melissa. My sisters and I were all in pain, but she seemed to be feeling it more than any of us, because she'd lived the closest geographically to my parents when they were alive, and now that they'd passed she felt like she was the furthest away from them.

I walked into my living room, looked at the photos of Mom and Dad, and said, "Please, folks, if you can, reassure Melissa, okay?"
I knew of nothing else I could do except... go back to working on my show. But even though I tried to stay focused, I found it nearly impossible to concentrate. Finally, I gave up, and decided to do something I had put off for too long.

I drove to Chester's grave for the first time, and put some flowers at his tombstone. His inscription read, "Looks like my chess clock finally ran out!" Even after his death, he was still making people laugh.

I drove back home in a much better mood, and just as I got in the door, the phone rang. It was Melissa, and she was borderline hysterical.

"Eddie, you won't believe it. Oh, my God!," she shouted.

"What's wrong?"

"Nothing! Can you hear that?"

Through the receiver, I could make out the faint ringing of a bell.

"Yeah, what is that?"

"After we hung up, I was sort of moping around the house for almost an hour, feeling sorry for myself. Then, just about five minutes ago, I asked Mom and Dad out loud to please give me some sort of sign. And I swear, the bells in the church across the street started ringing, and haven't stopped."

Wow, this was weird. It was a Saturday afternoon, and the bells at that church only ring on Sundays and Holy Days. There was no reason for them to be ringing now, except...

"Melissa, is there a function going on there or something?"

"No, it's completely dark. There is nobody there!"

I laughed. "Except for Mom and Dad, huh?" Melissa began sobbing, but they were the proverbial tears of joy. She said she finally felt that everything was going to be okay.

After Melissa and I hung up, I wandered into my living room and plopped down on the couch. Man, what a crazy year and a half it had been. There was a lot of loss involved. Losing people I loved, some through breakups, and more tragically, some through death. Losing faith, at least at times. Losing a sense of purpose.

However, the year held many gains as well. I gained new insight into others, and especially myself. I found purpose in my life, a purpose that had actually been there all along, but I hadn't recognized as such: making others laugh. It's the long-sought selfless side of my career as a comedian.

I finally came to believe that a sense of humor is indeed 'part of the soul,' as Mom's friend Mrs. Angie had put it, and thus, has meaning. Because creating comedy had always been something that came somewhat easily to me, I'd made the mistake of underestimating its importance, and trivializing its potential for making this world a better place.

I also gained the discovery that I can handle things I never would have guessed I could handle, from carrying out my parents' final wishes to comforting my family, no matter what the duress. Through Mom and Dad's struggles, as well as my own, I've gained new respect for people's ability to find the courage to battle the obstacles that are inevitable in this life.

I stared at the chessboard in my living room. No, the pieces still haven't been moved by my mom, but I realized that perhaps I'd been so intent on seeing the specific sign I'd asked for, I'd been missing the real signs that were happening all around me.

I've also come to realize that the conflict between having "down home" values and a high-powered career is something many people deal with, whether it's Hollywood or Wall Street or the local DA's office. For a long time, the city of Pittsburgh had been a sort of "family values" Valhella in my mind. Only recently had it become clear that it was the sense of community that was truly calling to me, not the city itself. And a sense of community can be nurtured in any town, even a city as big as LA, as long as I'm willing to make the effort.

I now know that if I just keep my own values, the proper direction will always reveal itself. Especially if I keep "my eyes, and ears, and heart open," as a wise woman once told me.

Truly, the world is filled with "unmoved chess pieces," signs that we've all asked for but don't receive, and we're all looking so hard to see what we've "demanded" that we miss the signs we're constantly being given all around us.

For me, life is the ultimate chess game. As long as I play the position as it actually is, instead of wishing it was different, I'll do just fine. And just because I don't see something doesn't mean it's not there.

★★★★★★★★★★★★

I walked out my front door and crossed the street to where I'd parked my car. I noticed something flapping in the wind under the driver's side windshield wiper. It was a piece of the honey bears stationary, on which was scrawled the words: *It's just as inappropriate to park on*

the street ACROSS from my house as it is to park directly in front of my house!!"
I laughed. I was home. Does anybody need some fully assembled, high quality boxes?

EPILOGUE

Late October 2010. "Daddy, how do you play this game?" My four-year-old daughter stood pointing at the chess board in the living room.

"Well, honey, it's a little complicated," I demurred.

"Will you teach me?" she persisted. I smiled. "Of course. Have a seat."

She boosted herself up on the chair behind the white pieces. "Okay, well, you get to go first," I began. Before I could expound any further, she picked up a pawn and pushed it several squares forward. "Is that a good move?" she asked. "It sure is," I enthused, "And now you---" I stopped suddenly, as a strange feeling hit me like a thunderbolt.

"Are you okay, Daddy?" asked the sweet face across the board.

"Yes, yes, I'm great. Thank you for moving that chess piece for me!" I answered, beaming.

"You're welcome," said my daughter, Margaret.

Made in the USA
Las Vegas, NV
19 June 2023